The
Inconvenient
Child

dee mcquesten

Happy Reading!

The complexity of our journey through life

and our faith is part of the meaning of our existence

and everything we value..... anonymous

Blessings,

Lee McQuestion

This book is dedicated to the three finest educators I have the privilege of knowing. These extraordinary educators teach not only the intellect of their charges, but reach into their hearts and souls, for the very first time, to demonstrate what unconditional non-judgmental love looks like. Greg Boyle refers to it as "Boundless Compassion."

Gregory Boyle, S.J., Jesuit Founder of Homeboy Industries, Los Angeles. Greg's front door entrance to Homeboy reads: "Assists At-Risk and Formerly Gang-Involved Young Men and Women to Become Contributing Members of Our Community"

Kaaren Andrews, Washington Director, Center for High School Success; Principal for 9 years of the Academy for traumatized and marginalized teens in Seattle's Columbia City;

L. Patrick Carroll, a dedicated educator and Jesuit Priest for 44 years, taught at Seattle University, 10 years of high school at Tacoma's Bellarmine Prep, Oregon's Jesuit High, and Holy Names Academy in Seattle. Pat has written 9 books, taught and lectured on the West Coast, throughout Canada, and in Africa; then patiently tutored me for more than two decades.

Table of Contents

Preface

Psychologists consistently maintain that the first 7 years of life are most determinate of a person's future. No one's life more substantiates this assertion than that of dee McQuesten, the most resilient person I know. Most know her as vibrant, dynamic, creative, relentless in pursuing what she believes and protecting those she believes in. She is also a wounded healer, whose earliest years provided a buffer against the next pain -ridden decades, evolving into a person who has carved out a life of much love and enormous public service.

Among the saddest small human stories I have heard in my 8 decades is the story of dee's 7th birthday.

At 10 months old dee was deemed an "inconvenient child" by her mother of birth and surrendered to, then adopted by, her maternal grandparents – a most loving, nurturing educated couple as this story will flesh out. Until her 7th birthday, August 10, 1948, dee was surrounded and nourished by her grandparents – known, by her, as, simply Gran and Grandpa, terms dee thought meant mom and dad.

On the afternoon of that birthday, the small child noticed a deep sadness in her parents, scarcely able to look at her and busy about other tasks. In the afternoon a car pulled up to the summer cabin in Rimrock. Two people whom dee had never seen emerged from the car. dee's Gran, with halting voice and teary eyes, summoned up the courage to tell her:

"Diane Dear, this is your **real** mother and her new husband. They are going to take care of your for now, but you can come home every summer. Grandpa and I will write to you all the time."

dee was placed in the car with little more explanation and driven off by these strangers to Seattle who smoked cigarettes, fist-fought, screamed, threw beer bottles and cigarettes out the car windows all the way to Seattle.

For the next 11 years, from 2nd grade through high school, dee lived through each school year with this couple, longing for summer and home to come.

People who knew dee in those school years would never have guessed what she was living, rarely spoken to without a raised, angry voice, rarely allowed a social life, never having any friends into her home, but still engaged and successful in school, holding down a variety of jobs, learning to play the viola, taking up tennis and, almost always, pictured with a smile on her face, despite the pain in her heart.

This book will fill in many details of those years, but to appreciate them, one must note the resilience contained.

This resilience carried on throughout her life. Working her way slowly through the University of Washington over 9 years, despite a dreadful start and the need to support herself and a husband throughout them all. Able to graduate despite unbelievable odds, while surviving and eventually escaping a marriage that entailed mostly being ignored, but often abused.

Then the halcyon years between marriages, a marvelous year at Harvard, a variety of jobs, a sailboat, varied, even astounding dates, lots and lots of tennis – but alone, longing for a family, fighting against numerous ingrained prejudices to establish the first downtown day-care in Seattle (or any downtown in the nation) partially so she could, if need be, adopt a child while working full time. Her own resilience helped initiate a single caring place that would eventually lead to many, many services for working parents, especially nursing mothers; now celebrating 42 successful years.

This ability to bounce back and begin again led dee slowly into a second marriage, and a child after she was forty. Through 14 years of family life, she tried to balance the joy of a motherhood with the misery of marriage to a consistently absent spouse – years in which resilience was a daily challenge. Again, while carrying this dual challenge, dee started a neighborhood newspaper, helped launch the now incredibly successful TreeHouse for Kids, aiding foster children throughout the state, and was part of the Seattle Art Museum Supporters that helped raise funds for Seattle's downtown Museum and sculpture park, along with serving on 6 additional non-profit boards.

This ability to trust and start over led dee to surrender this dysfunctional family, and, on her own again, without a dime to her name, care for a child, start a business, and move into the final, far more peaceful stage of her life.

This book, with stories that entertain, delight, and sometimes painfully touch your heart, will flesh out this slim outline, of the life of a woman I most admire, a woman who has, despite all medical expectations, kept me alive for more than two decades. This most inconvenient child has been for me a necessary helpmate, a best friend, treasured wife.

L. Patrick Carroll May, 2020

Introduction

Why did I write this book? Well, obviously for myself, to get outside all that is "in" – to know my own story by telling it to myself.

I also had two populations of readers in mind. First: Child Psychiatrists, MSW's, anyone who works with abused children. For decades we have heard that the first 6 or 7 years of a child's life establishes their adult stability or lack thereof.

I was adopted at 10 months old and ripped away from my adopted family on my 7th birthday. But the love from that 6 years and 2 months has sustained me and kept me somewhat whole. My story substantiates the normative assertion. That 6 years and 2 months of unconditional love built within me, thanks to Gran and Grandpa, the resilience I needed to become a productive adult living a purpose-driven life.

Second, for the very large adoption culture in this country. My story raises the serious question of presuming that an adopted child should often be returned to a birth family. It is also a mistake to believe that abuse primarily takes place in impoverished families. I was from a prominent, affluent, educated visible Seattle and Yakima family; my story is not that unique.

I believe this book, with all its stories, its evidence of growth and regression, of mistakes and delight, could serve as a kind of textbook for colleges and universities dealing with issues of the importance of our early years and the challenges of adoption.

I write this book, also, because I have spent most of my life believing other people were more valuable than I and trying to catch up, shape up, measure up. This story helps me, and perhaps others, realize it's okay to just be myself. Everyone else, after all, is taken! Emerson maintained that if we can tell well any individual's experiences we will always touch on the universal; all our stories are similar. We learn who we are by hearing other's stories.

I have received three great compliments in my life: A few years ago, when I visited Virginia MacDonald, who lived across the lane from us at Rimrock, said "Why Diane, if I couldn't see your face, I would think you were your Grandmother. You are just like her!" There is no one I would rather be more like.

David Skinner, Jr., at a dinner party in my home on Lake Washington Boulevard, once said "dee, this is the warmest home I have ever been in." I hope that's always true wherever I live.

And my dear, now twenty year spouse, Paddy, says over and over, "Without you, I would have no reason to live. I never feel particularly well, and I would quit trying, but you constantly inspire me to keep living."

Psychiatrists are right. If you have 6 or 7 years of a loving, nurturing stable environment at the beginning, no matter how painful emotionally and physically abusive the next years may be, you can pull yourself together and build a good life as an adult.

Here is my story!

Author's Note

All of the stories in this book are true.

Some names have been changed.

CHAPTER ONE

The Inconvenient Child Discovers Her Birth Mother

Gran, the only mother I had known 'til the day following my seventh birthday, seemed very busy that morning, preoccupied, distracted, around our mountain cabin in Rimrock, Washington, below the White Pass ski area.

Before lunch a strange (no, bizarre) looking woman appeared with an equally weird man and began throwing my clothes and books into the back seat of a beige Chevrolet sedan.

Gran and Grandpa were both crying. I had never seen Grandpa cry. Gran had cried once, hard, when she spanked me, ever so lightly.

I asked what was going on. Gran said, "Diane Dear, I cannot keep you from your real Mother." I replied, "YOU are my Mother!"

Apparently my birth-mother wanted to re-marry – a man who said he would marry her only if they retrieved me from my Grandparents' home so he could have a family. Scotty Spirk, a Boeing Engineer, couldn't have children; I was the pawn in their relationship, a deal breaker.

Even though they had legally adopted me, My Grandparents feared arguing with Rosemary, my birth-mother, who had, as I would soon discover, a violent temper, fueled by alcohol and drugs.

Gran and Grandpa, at 55 and 77 years, were too old to withstand a major confrontation, particularly with Grandpa's fragile heart.

This newly arrived woman was the oddest appearing female I had yet seen in my seven years. She had died black hair with exposed roots, ankle bracelets, noisy gold and beaded arm bracelets up above her elbows, with dangling earrings so enormous they bounced off her shoulders, bright red nail polish on fingers and toes and a blouse that was falling off both shoulders. Her lipstick was painted bright red up under her nose, beneath long flapping, barely glued-on eye lashes.

She was loud, harsh and more than slightly drunk.

This flamboyant couple simply tossed me into the back seat of their car and began racing across the mountain pass to Seattle, while drinking beer out of brown quart bottles, smoking and tossing cigarettes and matches out the windows, yelling, yahooing and fighting at the top of their lungs.

I was terrified!

I was wrenched from a home in which no one drank alcohol. In fact, no one was allowed to even bring alcohol in, as Grandpa's mother had (in his estimation) died at 105 of alcoholism, which embittered him. (Really!)

Though they did not fight with their daughter, Rosemary, Grandpa had negotiated a deal: they could take me to Seattle for the school year, but every June when school let out, my grandparents would pick me up and bring me home for the summer. While choking on tears, Grandpa carefully explained this arrangement which would provide my survival. Grandpa's large black Buick was packed up and ready to go. He was going to drive Gran to the Grand Canyon for a vacation. They were going to take some time off and travel around a bit and go visit my sister, Emmy, who was working in Seattle and brother, Joey, a student at the University of Washington, with a wife and little boy.

Frantically Homesick

To this little girl, torn from everything familiar, Seattle was a shock. My birth mother and, now, step-father lived in a tiny studio apartment on the back side of a building in the University District. Without a bedroom, I slept, and basically lived, in a closet on a Murphy bed.

It was hard to breathe. For the first time since infancy I became a bed-wetter, a mere foreshadowing of things to come.

When my folks returned from their frequent long nights out and my bed was wet, they yanked me awake and out of bed, screaming and telling me what a bad girl I was. Usually, I had awakened to a wet bed long before they returned but had no idea how to fix the problem. I didn't know where the sheets were or how to change a bed. I was freezing cold and couldn't find dry jammies.

They say children are flexible and adjust easily. I wasn't. I didn't. I began to cry a lot. I had never been a crier. In fact, I had never cried before, except at sad funeral music; even when I didn't know the deceased. Now, I cried myself to sleep every night. When I cried on the Murphy bed, they yelled at me and shut the closet door. Breathing became almost impossible. I was used to a good night kiss from both Gran and Grandpa. Gran always knelt beside my bed to say prayers. Often Gran sang to me while she rubbed my back until I was asleep.

Tossing and turning, this little girl wondered, sometime aloud, how long was I stuck here? How did this happen? When could I go home? Who were these people? I wanted to go home. They fought, screamed, hit, and were drunk all the time. I had never seen violent or drunken behavior. I wanted to go home. I didn't understand what they were doing. I was scared out of my mind. I wanted to go home.

They were almost always gone at night. I was alone. A neighbor boy came by sometimes to check on me. He fed me a strange dinner — rice, which I had never had before. I didn't like the food. It was cold rice. I didn't like the people. I didn't like the neighbor boy/baby-sitter. I didn't like the city or the harsh sidewalks that skinned my knees, hands and elbows. I wanted to go home.

Baby-sitter was a new idea to me. I had never had a "baby sitter" before. For one thing, I wasn't a baby — and why did I have to stay home? This new city wasn't any fun. I was not allowed to go anywhere but out on the small side porch steps.

All through those final endless first summer and fall weeks, where were the children? Nowhere. I had no one to play with. My parents went to work during the day. I was left home alone with instructions not to go outside the tiny apartment. It was lonely. And quiet. Nothing to do. I had read all my books several times. There were no more books. No books anywhere in this home. I was 7.

Where was Gran? What did she mean she was not my "real mother?" She WAS my real mother. Didn't she know that? How could she not know that? How could this bazaar woman just show up out of nowhere and claim to be my real mother?

What did "real mother" mean, anyway? Wasn't that the person who helped you dress for school and braid your hair? Didn't your real mother cook your breakfast and sew your clothes? Hike down to the creek with you after naps to go wading? Didn't your mother walk with you to the salt lick? Rock you while you wept for Suzy, your dead cat? Help you and grandpa make a grave and a cross for her? Kneel beside your bed at night to help you say prayers? Rub your back and sing to you to sleep? Read to you? Bake pies with you? Help you take a bath? Invite your friends in to play, and come for birthday parties, cook huge caramel popcorn balls on Halloween for your friends? Didn't such acts of love and caring for a small child constitute a "real mother"?

Was Gran gone? Who changed the rules?

This odd looking creature was not **MY** real mother!

How could they make this big a mistake? I had never seen her before; how could she be my "real mother"? She screamed at me for crying. No one had ever screamed at me before. She screamed at me for wetting my bed. She was terrifying. Her husband was scared of her, too.

Gran never screamed at me. She didn't scream at Grandpa. Grandpa didn't scream at either one of us. Something was wrong here. I wanted to go home.

This new pretend-mother said good girls didn't cry. The louder this woman screamed, the harder I cried until they began hitting me to make me stop. Nothing worked. I just wanted to go home. When could I go home?

Where was Grandpa? Would I never see him again? Grandpa said they were going on a vacation. What was a vacation? Would they pick me up on the way home from it? Did a vacation mean moving away? Where did they go? Why didn't they take me with them? I had never needed a "baby sitter" before. The three of us had always gone everywhere together; even at night. When my grandparents went out at night, it was to friends' homes for dinner. I always went, too. We were a family, the three of us. Now I was alone every night; eating strange food from a neighbor boy who didn't know how to cook. It was awful!

What about Joe Pope, who drove the school bus? How would he know where to pick me up for school? I was supposed to go back to Lower Naches Elementary for Second Grade this year. What about that? Didn't these people know that? Who were these people? I just wanted to go home.

New Home, Same Loneliness

In late fall, we moved to Magnolia Bluff where my mother and stepfather bought a home at the dead end of 33rd Avenue West. I still recall was our phone number – Alder 6662, a 4-party line. We paid $5,000.00 for the house with an over-sized yard.

Finally, there were other children: Kenny Wagner was across the alley. He used to say my birth mother smoked "skidderrettes." He thought smoking was an odd thing to do. Kenny's father had a butcher shop in the Pike Place Market where his mother, Barbara, also worked. I thought it was cool to go to the market and see his father, Jerry, on the main concourse. Kenny is now, and has been for many decades, a very successful professional photographer in Seattle.

Mary Barber and her father, Earl, lived directly across the alley from us, north of the Wagner's. Mary, whose father was a widower, re-married. My mother was angry because Kenny's mother,

Barbara, did not want to be friends with my mother. She said some people can only have one best friend and no one else. She was angry that Mr. Barber's new wife and Barbara were friends and they excluded my mother. It never occurred to my mother there were many reasons Mrs. Wagner and Mrs. Barber did not want to associate with her.

The Barber's had a piano in the basement off the alley. I went most days to play for an hour or two. I craved the piano and would have given anything to have one. My mother said we couldn't afford such things. I didn't understand how we could afford three cars and an enormous pink and white Cadillac Coupe DeVille, but no piano. Mary taught me to play Chopsticks!

Mary and Kenny both got bicycles for Christmas. They taught me and let me ride their bikes. I begged for one. My mother said we couldn't afford it.

Penny Johnson lived next to the Duncan's and adjacent to our sprawling huge back lawn. Penny and I used to trade cards at a time when doing so was the rage. Penny had a lot of beautiful equine photos. Penny also had a mild case of Cerebral Palsy. She walked "fancy."

Life was still lonely and hungry on Magnolia. My parents were gone partying every night. I was locked in a small 4×6 room from after school til they left. If I stayed outdoors, I was free to play in our yard and only in our yard. If I came indoors, I was not allowed in any part of the house, but that closet-sized small room. I was allowed out for breakfast and dinner, if we had dinner. Then locked up again.

They usually went for dinner at the Pier 91 Officers' Club or down to the Green Light Tavern on McGraw Street next to LeRoux's

Mens' Store. They came home drunk and fighting.

Sometimes they took me with them to the Green Light Tavern. Instead of parking on the main street, McGraw, in front of the tavern, where the street lights were lit, they parked the car in the dark unlit alley behind the tavern. I was warned not to get out of the car "or else!" I sat there, on occasion, for several hours shivering in the cold.

There were no blankets in the car; no heat of any sort. And no dinner.

Sometimes my birth-mother threw things. (For years, I had a sterling silver candelabra that was dented in several places from her throwing it down the alley at my step-father. I don't know why I kept it so long. Eventually, I gave it to the Good Will.)

Old Mr. Ole Olson lived next door south in a small cottage with a huge dahlia garden. He seemed ancient, somewhere between 80 and 90. Not very tall. I admired his garden. He had a thick Swedish accent, somewhat difficult to understand. One evening, just at dusk, when I was 9 or 10, I was standing on the back porch gazing at his quarter acre of dahlias when he said, "Come over to the fence." When I did, he grabbed me and kissed me on the lips! Stunned, I ran into the house and told my mother. She laughed: "Don't worry about it. He's harmless and very weak. He can't hurt you."

I never went out the backdoor again.

The Duncan's lived next door north. They also had an amazing garden of brilliant dahlias and roses. I went to Mrs. Duncan's to visit. They were a dear retired couple. Mrs. Duncan was concerned because I cried a lot. I assured her I was okay. She shouldn't worry.

The Macri's lived up the street. Sharon was a year or two behind me in school. I never got to know her very well. They weren't friendly. Understandably. We weren't a family anyone in their right minds would want to befriend.

Across the street from the Macri's lived the Art Valiton family. Mr. Valiton was an engineer at Boeing and a good father. Mrs. Valiton, after having one child, was told any more children might kill her, as her heart was very weak. She had three or four more children, all of whom, I think, had weak hearts. Several of them died; to my knowledge, only Bonnie, the first, is still living somewhere in Ravenna. My fondest memory of the Valiton family was of one Halloween when Mrs. Valiton invited me to come for a neighborhood childrens' party. She had a huge aluminum tub in the basement. We bobbed for apples. I hadn't seen that before. I thought it was great fun! I envied Bonnie, who had such kind parents. Her mother was a saint, the Valiton children were all terrific!

Next to the Valiton's was the Mark Tewis family. Velma. Mrs. Tewis, often came to our home covered with bruises. They had a lot of children. They eventually moved over to Magnolia Boulevard. She was the only neighbor who ever visited our home.

The Parsons, with two children, Nancy and Marianne, lived across the street on the southwest corner of 33rd and Bertona. Mr. Parson played his radio on the front porch every Saturday listening to Leo Lassen's commentary for the Seattle Rainiers Baseball game or the Brooklyn Dodgers while he mowed and trimmed the yard. Mrs. Parson used to bring over clothes for me, as Nancy and Marianne were a couple years older than me and taller. One day she brought over a huge box of beautiful party dresses, of which I still have pictures.

I was thrilled with them. Gran used to make beautiful dresses for me, but they were all school dresses, except every Easter when she sewed a new Easter coat and a special Easter dress. Gran's dresses were all embroidered and hand appliqued/embroidered. One of her dresses is pictured on the cover of this book. I wish I had saved one. Grandpa gave Gran $12 a month allowance; she spent all of it on sewing material for my clothes and my books. I want to go home!

deedee moving to Seattle August 11, 1948; day after 7th Birthday Party at Rimrock

CHAPTER TWO

Home

How did I get into this scarey situation, away from home? A brief history:

My mother was 18 and my father was 17 when they decided to get married (both barely Yakima High School Graduates). My mother had only one quarter of university at Texas A & M. They ran away, knowing my grandparents would disapprove. My Great Uncle, David McQuesten, Grandpa's brother, authorized their marriage license in Seattle.

My birth mother hated children with a passion, but OOPS... I was born anyway, 18 months later in Providence Hospital. We lived in a small apartment complex north of Yesler Way at 120 14th Avenue, Seattle's hardscrabble Central District. The apartment building, still there, has recently been renovated for condominiums, which are currently selling for $180,000!

My birth father, I am told, was at Seattle University on a music scholarship, working at the nearby Safeway as a box boy. My mother dropped out of Texas A & M after one quarter. She was working at the Varsity Theater on University Way as an usher. She had an outfit. She was emotionally unsuitable for motherhood, an alcoholic and pill popper. She claimed there was never enough money to feed me, so she stole milk off the neighbors' back porches in our apartment building. She told me later that my birth father often shook me to make me stop crying, which didn't work. (I didn't believe her, as she was the violent one.) Eventually, I acquired scarlet fever; hence, my life-long heart murmur.

After a brief, stormy time enduring my mother's screaming and violence, my birth father left and joined either the Army or the Air Force. I was 6 months old. My mother shouted and complained to everyone that I was "inconvenient!"

Fortunately for me, my maternal grandparents stepped in and adopted me. Grandpa was 71 and Gran was 49. Grandpa, an attorney, was optimistic that Gran, a retired nurse still raising two children, could handle one more, me. Emma was 14; Joey was 12; aunt, uncle/sister, brother. I was 10 months.

Luckily, I went with them to our Tieton Drive home that Gran designed and Grandpa had built for her in Yakima in 1920. Grandpa was in the Washington State Senate. Gran looked after the family.

I need to tell you what that home was like and why I missed it so.

One of my earliest memories of Tieton Drive was hiding in the big grandfather clock in the downstairs hallway during my nap so Gran couldn't find me, but she always did.

One of my earliest memories of our home at 2012 Tieton Drive was Joey playing his harmonica while the big Christmas tree was being decorated in the dining room by Grandpa high upon a ladder.

I remember the small wooden kitchen stool where I sat while Gran was cooking – the stool still resides in our kitchen today. She gave me a table knife and a bar of soap to carve while she cooked. The kitchen was so large I tricycled around with my black and white leather panda on the handle bars.

I remember my first "Diane Dear" lecture when I dunked my panda in the washbowl for a bath on the steps to the cellar. I was 3. I smeared him with a bar of soap. Gran discovered me, so I didn't get to finish his bath!

I recall the big swing in the yard. Gran was surprised when, one day, while I was swinging, my paternal Grandmother, Mary Hawkins, came by to give me a rag doll she had made.

I still have the photo taken on the kitchen steps the day Gran taught me to tie my shoes.

Neither we nor our neighbors locked our doors; it was a safe town in a safe era. Frequently, when a neighbor, Mrs. Sinsel, left her house, I climbed the high steps leading to her kitchen door and sneaked in to visit with her bright-feathered parrot, who would talk away to his young uninvited, but apparently welcome, visitor. Mrs. Sinsel didn't know of these visits.

I remember how high each step was from our porte co-chere up to the front terrace of our home on Tieton Drive. I remember the small pine tree, now 80' high, that Grandpa planted to shade my baby carriage for naps.

I remember how kind and soft spoken Gran was, a stunning beauty and shockingly thick black silky hair, her warmth, her slow, graceful, but deliberate walk. In the 40 years she was my best friend and my nurturing mother, she never raised her voice, always with her endearing "Diane Dear." Grandpa and the rest of the family always called me "deedee."

Joe and Anna Slavin were my folks' best friends. We went to their home or they to ours for most Sunday dinners.

The Martin's lived kitty-corner across the street, next to Fifes. Mrs. Martin, Donny and Glenny, looked after me whenever Gran had to go to St Elizabeth hospital to see Grandpa, who had several heart attacks. When I was three, Mrs. Fife, next door to Martin's, washed my mouth out with soap in her bathroom sink for saying a bad word; I told Donny Martin to "shut up."

One day, when I was 4, Bobby Armstrong (who lived in the brick home next door south of us) and I decided to get married. We were four. We took my big green wicker doll carriage and my doll, crossed Tieton Drive and began walking. We got half way up the hill in front of Franklin Junior High when Grandpa drove up, asking where we were going. We brought him up to speed on our plans.

When we returned to the house, Grandpa, apparently not amused, tied a very long, probably 15', rope to the willow tree out back in front of the garages and tethered the other end to me, lest I wander off again. I don't know what became of Bobby Armstrong. We had a good thing going.

I remember, one day shortly after that, when, I decided to cross the street to Fife's on my own. Our fourteen year-old black cocker spaniel, Tippy, grabbed hold of my coveralls' shoulder strap and pulled me back up onto the lawn.

Rimrock and Tale Telling Paint

"Home" also meant the time we spent at Rimrock, always in summer, later year around since Grandpa was having heart attacks with increased frequency. Doc England told him he had to take a break from the Senate and politics or he would die very soon, within three months. So, from age five, we spent most of the year at our summer home below the White Pass Ski area and Rimrock Lake.

Halloween, was my favorite celebration because when I lived with my family, at Rimrock, Gran always made huge caramel popcorn balls on our ancient antique wood stove for all of my school and neighbor friends. I was very proud that we had the best treats. I felt so important.

Old Joe Pope, our Rimrock to Naches school bus driver, rarely sober and infinitely patient with our noisy crowd, drove us around from cabin to cabin each Halloween night, so that each child's family could participate in the festivities. When we arrived at our cabin, (the last one up on the highway route), I was bursting with pride.

Life was not easy for Gran, who had no household help at the cabin. She cooked on an ancient wood stove. It was important to her that clothes be washed, starched and ironed properly. She washed, bent way over, on a small rippled wash board in the bath tub. She rolled everything in a bowl of starch to set over night, then ironed them with a flat iron heated on our wood stove. I still have that funny little iron, now my door stop.

On Thursdays, the iceman brought a huge chunk of ice for the icebox on the screen porch. Gran canned peaches, pears, apricots, tomatoes, cherries, jellies, jams and other forgotten goodies on the old wood kitchen stove in the heat of summer. I can still see in my memory the sweat pouring off her red face onto her worn faded hand-made apron for three or four weeks each July and August. I remember her swollen legs and feet. Sill, faithfully each night, she knelt beside my bed on the rough-hewn wooden floor teaching me prayers.

I still pray on my knees as Gran modeled for me.

Grandpa's heart worsened. His doctors sent him to the Mayo Clinic in Minnesota for heart surgery. He disappeared. Monty Hadzer, the Intake and Yakima River Waterfall Caretaker over at the Rimrock Dam, had the only telephone in the area. Monty came one day to say the FBI and State Police all across the nation were searching for Grandpa. He vanished the day after his heart surgery.

Grandpa had sponsored the Washington State Teachers' Pension Bill in the Senate, about which many folks were angry. Despite political opposition, he felt strongly there should be retirement money for teachers. Hence, the strong law enforcement involvement in the search for him.

We heard no word for five long days. Gran was frantic. Then, one day, he came hobbling up the road from the highway, his chest and stomach all bandaged up. We soon learned that he had asked at the Registration when he checked into the Mayo Clinic, what the cost of the surgery, anesthesia, room, and ancillary costs would be. He always paid cash up front, as he didn't believe in insurance, or credit of any kind.

The morning after his surgery, he had risen, dressed and left the hospital. He took a cab to the Rochester Train Station and, after the days-long train ride to Yakima, hitch-hiked home from the Yakima station 30 miles to Rimrock. He insisted he had a better nurse at home than any nurse at Mayo, so he wasn't going to waste his time nor money on foolishness! I remember Grandpa lying listlessly in the big brass bed for days, after his return, while Gran changed his dressings and brought him meals, changed his bloody bandages and brought him back to life.

This, my wonderful early home, was not just immediate family. At

Rimrock, we had company every night for dinner and lots more folks on Sundays.

About 4:30 each afternoon Gran sent me across the road to Joe Alcorn's (a retiree) or over to Glen and Elizabeth Cooley's inviting them to come for supper. Glen, the local Sheriff, mowed the lawns for the summer cabins and, with his wife, ran the local Rimrock grocery – mostly one glass case of candy bars, a few loaves of bread, milk and some pop) and a gas pump on the highway.

In those pre-TV days, people used to visit. On Sundays Grandpa insisted that everyone who stopped in to visit, stay for dinner. Sundays became a miniature collection of America at the time—a kind of Saturday Evening Post gathering – old Doc and Mrs. Braden from next door , Doc England, Jr. and Mamie England from town, Doc England, Sr., the Slavin's, the Eichelberger's, Cooley's, Dan and Virginia McDonald, directly across the road; and most amazingly, looking back, the Honorable Justice William O. Douglas of the U.S. Supreme Court, who lived north of us in Goose Prairie. Justice Douglas, we recall as the court's most avid liberal, while Grandpa was a conservative Republican State Senator, still but they had enormous, healthy respect for each other. Family lore had it that Justice Douglas would occasionally come by Sunday dinner, also.

Before those suppers, every Sunday morning we drove into Yakima for Church services at the Yakima First Baptist Church. Gran, raised Catholic, attended Grandad's Baptist church dutifully and without complaint. Frequently, after church we attended the Grange, Shriner's or political picnics in the Yakima Parks, to which we always took fried chicken, a cake and potato salad.

When we arrived home, Grandpa took a chicken or two out of the coop under my bedroom window and cut off its head on the side yard chopping block, used primarily for kindling. I still visualize those chickens running headlessly around the yard. It became Gran's challenge to de-feather, disembowel, prepare, then fry in enormous quantities.

We had a beautiful large fluffy white cat, Suzy, who had a litter of 6 kittens. The biggest trauma of my early life came when one morning Suzy didn't come in for breakfast. I remember finding her stiff, cold body near Braden's next door porch. Our neighbor, Mrs. Braden, had put out some mouse poison, which Suzy unwittingly ate. Gran took her six little kittens, too young to survive without Suzy, in a gunny sack down the hill to Wildcat Creek. I watched her hold the sack, filled with kittens, under the freezing cold water for a long, long time. I was devastated.

We trudged up the road above Eichelberger's cabin, Suzy in tow, in a large brown gunny sack that had housed our potatoes, and dug a grave for her, surrounding it with some pretty rocks, placing a large rough-hewn cross Grandpa had made for her at the head of Suzy's grave. Returning to the cabin, I sat in Gran's lap and cried for at least two endless hours while she rocked me in her high back beautiful old hand-carved rocking chair that Grandpa's grandfather had carved in New England. (which Morgan now owns.)

Dan and Virginia McDonald, across the road, were hunters. Their home featured animal heads all over the walls, drawn from their various safaris. The McDonalds came to Rimrock, only in the winter to hunt deer, bringing a large entourage with them.

The Don Keith family, who operated the Keith and Keith Funeral Home in Yakima, lived in the cabin behind us, next to our hillside garage. Royal and his little sister, Lindel, were frequent summer visitors. Lindel and I were inseparable when they were at their cabin.

Pingrey's lived behind and next to Keith's, one door east. They

didn't come often, but when they did, there were many of them
– legion!

My bedroom was on the west side of the house above Wildcat
Creek. I went to sleep at night to the sound of the babbling creek.
Each afternoon, after my nap, Gran took me down the scary, steep,
8" narrow dirt path about 100 yards down to the creek where she
sat on a huge rock while I went wading, giggling and playing in loud
rushing, tumbling water.

I loved to visit Myrtle and Johnny Eichelberger across and up the
road one cabin east of Joe Alcorn. Once, when Johnny Eichelberger
gave their cabin a fresh coat of forest green paint, Gran urged me
not to go up the lane and bother him while he was painting. I could
not resist seeing the new paint job. That afternoon, while Gran
was otherwise occupied in the kitchen, I snuck out of my nap, me-
andering up the hill to visit with Johnny while he painted. Woops.
. . . I slipped off the lawn into the garden and down a short slope,
brushing my striped tee shirt left sleeve and strap of my coveralls
with green paint.

Told not to bother Johnny, I knew I was about to be scolded.
Thinking to outsmart everyone, I climbed down the steep dirt path
to the creek, took off my shirt and coveralls and tried, fruitlessly,
to wash off the paint. When my cleaning efforts failed, I threw my
shirt and coveralls in the creek. I climbed back up the hill in my
underwear and sensible brown shoes and socks. I returned to the
cabin and, ever so quietly, sneaked past Grandpa, who was reading
the afternoon paper in the living room, back to my bedroom where
I hid safely under the covers, feeling vastly relieved. I had avoided
detection!!!

A very short time later, some fisherman farther down the Yakima
River found my clothes.

The next thing I knew, Gran was in tears, pulling the covers off me, explaining how everyone in the whole area had a search party out looking for me, combing the river and creek banks. The whole grotto of cabins and the crew from the Forest Ranger Station had been looking frantically for a missing, perhaps now drowned, four-year-old, while I, after my big ordeal, was sleeping peacefully, well hidden under the covers in my big green ornate iron bed. Gran and Grandpa had initially looked in my bedroom, but didn't see me under the thick bulky hand-made quilts.

Grandfather went out to call off the search that, by then, had expanded for miles down the Yakima River.

The whole neighborhood and others from the search party – about thirty huge adults – filled our living room, witnesses to my first spanking. As I sprawled across her lap, Gran was crying, saying it hurt her worse than me! Grandpa stood close by, supporting, but never doing the spanking.

After that, this little five-year-old girl, trudged up to Johnny Eichelberger,'s to tell him I was sorry that I bothered him while he was painting his cabin. He needed no apology, so happy I was alive!

A Bear Problem and a Big Ass Whoopin'

I remember vividly, the quiet summer day that Monty Hadzer took Gran, Grandpa and I through the underside/inside of the Rimrock Dam above the Yakima River under Rimrock Lake. It was a cold, dark, drippy, ginormous cave. Of even more interest to me was watching Mrs. Hadzer in her yellow kitchen using her old Iron-Rite to iron Monty's shirts. She sat down while she ironed; she could do a whole shirt in 2 minutes.

Monty's caretaker home just below the Rimrock Dam had a tennis court on the grounds. I never saw anyone use it, but later learned my mother, Joey and Em played there frequently, presaging my life-long love of tennis.

We had a problem with bears for a time. During the night, bears came down the path between the Keith's and the Pingrey's, dumping over our garbage cans. This irritated Grandpa, beyond belief. He resolved to put an end to it. One night, he took a 2-by-4 out of the garage and hammered a large construction nail all the way through till it jetted out at least 2 inches. That night when Grandpa heard a bear rattle the garbage lid, he flew out the pantry screen door, whooped the bear on his rear end and sent him yelping back up the path into the woods.

None of the cabins ever had a bear problem again.

Once Joe Alcorn built a lovely looking pair of stilts for me with wide leather straps. The stilts were hard to walk on since the only roads around our grotto of cabins were rocky and uneven, but I persisted. Some years later, in one of my rare good memories of that time, I took those stilts back to Seattle where I pranced up and down our level sidewalk. I used to get blisters from the foot straps, but I didn't care. I loved those tall sharp looking stilts. They were extremely high. Joe had sanded, polished and varnished the wood til gleaming. You couldn't get that nice a pair of stilts at Montgomery Ward's Sporting Good Department in downtown Yakima. I was the luckiest kid ever!

I can still hear Joe telling me, on several occasions, his favorite saying: "deedee, there's more than one way to skin a cat," which seemed a scary thought. Did he really skin cats? I wasn't sure. Gran used to send me over to invite Joe for supper every night. (We had dinner at noon and supper at night, except on Sundays, when dinner was at 3:00.)

Sometimes Joe, who always wore his red plaid wool shirt – even in summertime, went up to Rimrock Lake and caught trout for supper. I was invited to go along, but I quit going because he wouldn't let me talk. No fun at all! Joe said if the fish heard us, they would stay away.

Most of my friends in those years were adults over 70. How I loved to visit and listen to their conversations, mostly on our expansive front porch/veranda, and around the dining room table.

Frequently in the afternoons, after my nap, Gran, Grandpa and I walked up the road past Eichelberger's and deep into the forest to check the salt licks – huge white 12" square cubic blocks of salt the Forest Rangers would put out on shorn tree stumps for the deer. Grandfather studied how worn the licks were to determine how many deer were around. We frequently saw deer in our front yard in the early morning, but never in the afternoon after the cabins were stirring as people were walking around. The deer were painfully shy and skittish, particularly the mother deer with new fawns.

Other days I climbed clear to the top of Rimrock Ridge high above the cabins with P.K. Hubbard (from the summer cabins in the Grotto across the highway). It was a dangerous climb across and up huge boulders. I rarely went alone, but, whenever I could talk some other child into it, off we'd go. The view was amazing. It felt like we were at the top of the world - so far away from everyone. We never feared wild animals or sliding boulders. We were invincible. Today, there is a road; you can drive all the way to the top of the ridge.

Shopping Sprees at the One-Counter Grocery

I remember the many times Gran sent me across the highway, over the bridge to the Cooley's store to buy bread and milk for supper.

Sometimes in the afternoons, Grandpa would open his old leather pocketbook (made of a piece of an elephant's ear) and give me a penny to spend at Cooley's for a green or orange sucker. I ventured off, after a careful explanation from Gran, "This, Diane Dear, is a nickel and this is a dime. Put your money in your pocket and give it to Elizabeth for a loaf of bread and a quart of milk." 15 cents in my coverall pocket. Gran trusted me. I liked to hang out atop the high old cement bridge over Wildcat Creek, watching the raging water about 50' below. After the depression, the bridge was built by President Roosevelt's WPA. One afternoon I dropped both my dime and my nickel off the edge of the bridge, as I playfully leaned over the edge, watching the water below. After as much lollygagging, procrastinating as long as I thought I could get away with, I had to go home and tell Gran I lost all her money. She went with me, climbing 100 yards down the steep, narrow dirt path, to look for the change in the roaring creek below the bridge - to no avail. Another scolding!

My credibility as a trustworthy five year old tumbled even farther after that when we went into town to shop. Gran made all of my clothes on her old oak treadle sewing machine. This particular day, she bought a new pattern and some fabric for me at Montgomery Ward. She put the fabric, her money, ($11.00 and some change) in a brown paper bag tied up with white string and gave it to me to hold onto while she did some other shopping.

In the '40's, all the women wore gloves, stockings, a hat and black sensible shoes when they went into town. Gran's gloves were white. Gran was very tall, so I barely came up to her glove. I turned around to look at something. When I turned back, I grabbed hold of a white glove; it was not Gran's. The woman left with my package with all of Gran's money inside. Another scolding. I was 5.

Funeral, Memorial Services and Picnics

Since many of Grandpa's friends were elderly, almost every Saturday, we went into town to either the Keith & Keith or Shaw & Sons Funeral Homes for friends' funerals. I cried at funerals because the music made me sad, even if the deceased was unknown to me. As he knew, literally, everyone in town, Grandpa stood outside after each ceremony and shook everyone's hand.

Our weekly shopping and banking trips to downtown Yakima were often on Saturdays for the funerals. While I was small enough, I used to ride in Gran's lap. When I was too big for her lap, I was re-located to the back seat. This was awkward because Grandpa liked to spit out the window while he was driving. The summer weather was hot in Eastern Washington, so all of the windows were open. Sometimes the spit would fly back and hit me in the face, which upset Gran. She would say, in her most exasperated tone of voice, "OH DOWE!!!

Birthdays were more fun. I clearly remember my 5th birthday. Gran always asked what kind of a cake I'd like – always gingerbread with thick white seven minute icing. No one made gingerbread or frosting like Gran. Everything came out of her kitchen, wonderfully, from scratch. On this memorable fifth birthday, Grandpa decided since it was a weekend and the loggers were not working, we should fetch some firewood for winter. We drove off into the hinterlands with a saw and a hatchet.

After hours of hard work getting wood and loading up the trunk, we stopped to visit some friends on the way back. When Grandpa introduced me, I proudly pronounced: "I am five today!" I thought everyone should know.

On one of our forays into the woods, a tick somehow burrowed into Grandpa's chest, even though he always wore long sleeved, long legged, heavy white flannel underwear, even in July and August. (And that was under his long sleeved white dress shirt and three-piece navy blue or brown pin-striped suit, fedora and gold pocket watch. He wore the same clothes to funerals that he did to saw wood in the forest or to read the evening paper (just before we listened to the evening news – Gabriel Heater "Blows His Horn." A constant in my life was G. Dowe McQuesten's formal attire; always a proper New Englander.)

I recall how expertly, but with much discomfort to Grandpa, Gran extracted that disease- carrying very dangerous tick with a burning flame and a knife.

We took many weekend excursions to stockpile firewood for our kitchen wood stove and living room potbelly's upcoming winter. By October we had wood piled high. We never ran out. Despite his fragile heart, Grandpa sawed, chopped and splintered all the wood himself.

Christmas Eve Lock-down

When we lived at Rimrock during the school year, our school bus driver, how old Joe Pope (though, probably 30, he seemed reeeee-ally old to me) would care for me. Each winter morning he hiked up the lane to our cabin from the highway to carry me out, arms stretched over his head, through the deep 4' snow. We left at 7:30 a.m. (after a huge bowl of mush or Cream of Wheat smothered in brown sugar and butter in front of the pot belly stove). We did not return 'til 5:00. Joe had to drive for more than an hour into Naches to the Elementary School and take the Arneson children from the Ranger Station to Naches High School, 30 miles each way. Going down the mountain highway was pretty quiet for us sleepyheads, but coming home we'd sing and carry on like there was no tomorrow.

We saw a lot of Christmas decorations. For our living room at the cabin. Grandpa always cut down a large fir tree from the forest behind the cabin. The trees in the stores downtown had snow on them. All we had were popcorn strings, colored balls and tinsel. I could fix that. One afternoon, again while Grandpa was reading the paper in the big oak rocker, and Gran was busy fixing dinner, I marched down the front steps with great anticipation to create a wonderful surprise for them. I carted load after load after load of snow – since we had more than plenty outside – on old news-papers, carefully layering the pure white snow evenly on the our Christmas tree branches as far up as I could reach. Again, I was sooo **BUSTED**! Grandpa quickly scraped off all the snow he could (in between yards of tinsel) into a brown cardboard box and car-ried it back outside and down the front steps to its rightful place on the front lawn. The difference was carefully explained to me between real snow and cotton snow. Also, Grandpa patiently ex-plained how dangerous it was to run up and down the front porch steps because there were several feet of snow on the roof that could slide and quickly bury me.

Another mis-guided adventure came shortly after this, on Christmas Eve. Gran locked the front door as she always did at bedtime. But she had been reading Christmas stories to me about Santa coming down the chimney. The stovepipe on the potbelly providing living-room heat was clearly too skinny for any Santa to navigate. The same with the big wood stove in the kitchen. Despite much frantic, urgent pleading on my part, Gran simply did not understand that Santa would be locked out. That night, I waited for both of them to fall asleep, then stealthily sneaked past Grandpa's open bedroom door and unlocked the front door. This was particularly tricky, as

Gran slept with me because Grandpa snored so loudly. It worked. Santa came and, apparently, no one was the wiser.

To Be or Not To Be – An Accidental Liar?

Shortly after my 5th birthday it was time to start school – a big deal. Grandpa took me on my first day to register at Lower Naches Elementary. I think my teacher's name was Miss Thiene. We went off by ourselves, Gran waving in the front yard. Grandpa pushed the car backward out of the garage. We had a big black Buick sedan, which I watched Grandpa crank up with a front end hand crank until the motor roared, then off we went!

The beginning didn't go well. As we walked across the school lawn, a paper airplane came flying past me. I hurriedly collected it and gave it to the boy who tossed it. He yelled at me that they were having a contest and I should not have picked it up! Oh dear! Well, I came here to learn! I still remember our first book, <u>See Dick Run</u>; <u>See Jane Run</u> It had lots of great pictures of Dick and Jane chasing their dog, Spot. This was monumental, as reading was a very big thing in our family – and, now, I could do it! It wasn't hard after all. Miss Thiene was a nice teacher. We all liked her.

Before long, while waiting for the school bus, I discovered some children were roller skating on the school's tennis court after school. I talked/begged one of the children to lend me their skates, to let me try it. The skates had brown leather straps and a key to tighten the cleats around your shoe soles. Each time I tried it, I sprained my ankle. Then, Joe Pope would have to gather me up off the cement court and carry me to the school bus. When I arrived home, Gran wrapped it tight in a long brown Ace bandage and warned me to stay off the roller skates. But I couldn't do that. Anything athletic fascinated me. I was back at it and another sprained ankle. Finally,

I got the hang of it and learned to skate on one foot and do other nonsensical tricks, a stereotypical five-year-old tomboy.

My first Report Card so unsuccessful, no one could have anticipated my 1970 year at Harvard. I got in some serious trouble with Gran. One of the questions Miss Thiene asked us to answer on our own was "Do you always tell the truth? Do you sometimes lie?" Thinking through the question carefully, I answered maybe sometimes I told lies. I tried to explain to Gran that I didn't know everything yet, so some of the things I said might not be true. How was I to know? My second light spanking. And a lecture on how important it was to *always* be truthful. If I didn't know for sure, I shouldn't say anything.

The second half of first grade I attended McKinley Grade School in Yakima. We needed to be in town for a while for another hospitalization for Grandpa's heart. I remember the huge smock Gran made for our art projects out of one of Grandpa's white dress shirts.

Our teacher repeatedly told us not to eat the wet gooey clay. She said it so many times I became curious to know why we would want to. So I ate some. A lot. I found out clay reeeeeally constipates you – for days and days. The teacher called Gran and I got another lecture to go with my enormous stomach ache!

After our noon dinner and dishes, Gran took a bath and washed her hair (which came down to her waist) and put it up in a bun, put on a clean cotton dress, patted on some Yardley Powder and a tiny bit of medium pink lipstick, (with maybe a small dab on her cheeks as Grandpa did not approve of make up or jewelry.) A little bit of pink on Gran's cheeks was especially striking, as her eyes were a beautiful Grey blue and clear as a bell. No earrings. She wore a broche on her good dresses, suits and coats.

By the time she was finished, I was up from my nap and was given a choice of two caramels out of a small green handle-less woven basket. Gran sewed for a while as we listened to her two radio serials, "The Second Mrs. Burton" and "Our Gal Sunday." Then we'd climb down the long and dangerously narrow dirt path on the steep side of the hill below the cabin to wildcat Creek, about 100 yards below my bedroom window; Gran in her sensible canvas Granny shoes with 2" square heels, her white apron, and a large towel for me. Gran sat on a huge rock – the largest in Wildcat Creek, far below the over-arching Rimrock Bridge – towel in hand, patiently waiting while I splashed around freezing cold water, new run-off of melted snow from the Intake just above us far, far up the creek. Then Gran would spend the afternoon sewing – usually making me play and school clothes – before she began supper.

An Old-Fashioned Courtship

I talk so much about Gran and Grandpa; let me tell you more about them, before me.

There was quite a spread in my Grandparents' ages. Gran was 23 when they married; Grandpa was 56. Gran was the beautiful daughter of French Catholic Joseph LaPlante and Swedish Lutheran Emma Lundberg both hailing from San Francisco, later Puyallup, Washington. Joseph, one of the five LaPlante brothers, was an early Puyallup City Manager, then titled City Clerk. Emma died when Gran was five, of pneumonia. Gran was sent to San Francisco to live with Joseph's sister, Mary LaPlante Biss, and Mary's husband, Charlie Biss. After a period of time, the Biss's decided it would make more sense for the three of them to move north so the whole family could live together. Joseph missed his tiny daughter and she missed him.

George Dowe McQuesten, (known as G. Dowe because Grandpa didn't like his first name, George) was a staunch New Englander who had no R's in his vocabulary (hoss was horse....havad was Harvard). He was born with a fairly silver spoon in his mouth to an old New York/Connecticut/New Hampshire family. Grandpa's lineage was fascinating and powerful. His multi-great grandfather was William the Conqueror. His other multi-great Great-Grandfather, Matthew Thornton, was the final signature on the Declaration of Independence, representing New Hampshire. Family lore maintained that John Quincy Adams had married one of the McQuesten women. G. Dowe was part of the New York Morgan and Dow and Jones families. His mother dressed him in long curls and velvet suits with white lace collars. He hated his look. He desperately wanted to look like the other lads in the schoolyard. He and his mother fought constantly about his clothes and hair.

When he was 11, a tall fifth grader, G. Dowe ran away from home and lied about his age. Saying he was 15, he was able to find a job cutting railroad ties on the trans-continental railway across the U.S.

Upon completion of the railroad, G. Dowe was invited to ride across country on its maiden voyage. His assigned seat mate was a man named William Cody – "Buffalo Bill." Grandpa told wonderful stories about his conversations with Wild Bill as they crossed America on these ties he had worked so hard to cut.

After 6 months of cutting ties, G. Dowe realized that there must be something to having an education. He had only completed part of the 5th grade. G. Dowe bought an old Royal Typewriter and taught himself two-finger hunt-and-peck typing. He bought a shorthand book and memorized it on his two-hour walk to and from the railroad yard each day.

At seventeen, he decided, to go into politics.

G.Dowe hailed from a long line of powerful men: William the Conqueror, (1028 – 1087), the first Norman King of England; rendering me a distant cousin to Princess Diana of Wales, also a multiple great-granddaughter. In addition, Matthew Thornton (1714 – 1803), Physician, and one of 3 New Hampshiremen to sign the Declaration of Independence.

He began his political quest, quite logically to him, at the U.S. Department of the Interior.

The Administration thought it important that everyone on the staff be educated, an opinion with which G. Dowe fervently agreed, so he attended night school and obtained his GED, then continued on, earning his undergraduate degree from George Washington University, then continuing at G.W.U at night to complete his Law Degree and after that, a Post-LLB, all of which , as Grandpa proudly told me, were paid for, at President Cleveland s' request, either per by the White House budget and/or President Cleveland's personal funds!

Grandpa was an intelligent, motivated student. After a short stint practicing law, he was admitted to the Supreme Court of the District of Columbia.

When Cleveland lost the election to President Harrison in 1889, G. Dowe transferred over to the Department of Justice. In 1893 Cleveland ousted Harrison in the following election and G. Dowe returned to the White House.

In Cleveland's second term, just before the turn of the century, he sent G. Dowe out to the Washington Territory to be the Director of the Bureau of Indian Affairs, the BIA. G. Dowe quickly set about the awesome task of learning several separate Native American languages peculiar to the Pacific Northwest. His central proud accomplishment during his time in that post came when the Chief of the Leschi Tribe asked Grandpa to represent his son in a murder trial. Grandpa, an old-fashioned lawyer who vowed he would never represent anyone unless he was convinced they were innocent, got the Chief's son acquitted in a somewhat famous Washington State murder trial .

After that G. Dowe successfully ran for the Washington State House and ultimately the Washington State Senate from Tacoma and, later, from Yakima.

Though now a politician of sorts, G. Dowe was a bit of a wild hare. He bought the first motorcycle imported into Tacoma. Roaring around town one day in his customary three-piece pin striped suit and fedora, he hit a horse. The horse was not seriously injured, but G. Dowe, alas, broke his leg in three places. Into his Tacoma General Hospital room wafted a beautiful, serene nurse named Maybelle LaPlante. G. Dowe knew her father, Joseph, as they were political allies. For the next few days, while his leg was up in traction, he watched this stunning beauty float in and out of his hospital room. When he was released from the hospital, he called upon Joseph LaPlante, asking him if he would he give his daughter's hand in marriage, if G. Dowe could get a divorce from his current estranged wife.

G. Dowe and Ida McQuesten had been a most unhappy couple who fought constantly, had two children who had died, one at 6 months of pneumonia, the other at 18 months of unidentifiable infant death syndrome.

Divorce was an important decision in G. Dowe's life, since he once had much higher political ambitions. Divorce extinguished any chance of political advancement. G. Dowe sacrificed his political career, courted, and married the lovely Maybelle LaPlante.

They were married on Labor Day, September 1, 1919, at home, in Puyallup and set off for a unique honeymoon. At that time, Grandpa was Director of State Institutions. The wedding date was arranged so that Gran could accompany him on his obligatory annual rounds of the institutions he was overseeing. They did take one day in Victoria, B.C., and after, they stayed, for no expense, at State Institutions in Buckley, at Western State in Steilacoom, the penitentiary in Walla Walla, Purdy and and other similar, less than romantic venues. Grandpa, was a very thrifty Scot; fortunately for him, Gran was a good sport!

We have two lovely reproductions in our home they purchased on their Honeymoon in a Spokane antique shop: Raphael's "Madonna of the Chair" and Jean-Francois Millet's "The Angelus".

G. Dowe's first wife, Ida, was bitter and angry about the divorce. In a strange retaliatory move, she ran for a seat in the Washington State House largely on his name familiarity and stellar reputation as a cutting edge lawmaker and prominent lawyer. When Grandfather won his second Senate seat in Tacoma, he found that to every McQuesten Bill he introduced, Ida filibustered.

Soon Tacoma, with Ida's proximity, became intolerable. Grandpa moved his new wife to Yakima. Shortly after his arrival in Yakima, G. Dowe, along with some others, initiated a consortium to open a Grange so farmers could buy their supplies in bulk. He then went on to practice law in Yakima, buy several farms and orchards and develop/build several private residences. Life was good. G.Dowe practiced law for another 42 years; some years from his home office, until he died in 1965.

Life was frequently complicated for Gran, by grandpa's many irons in many fires. He often called between 2:00 and 3:00 in the afternoon, announcing he would be bringing people home for dinner, as many as 15 or 20 people, working on some legislative committee and needing to continue on into the night. Gran always made it work. Though She did have some household help in that era, her life was always chaotic was long as G. Dowe was involved in politics.

My only personal political memory was being scolded for sliding down the beautiful (and lengthy) brass banisters in the Olympia Capitol Dome Building! I embarrassed Grandpa and even my brother/uncle Joey, who was a Senate Page at the time, quite a polite young man, would never do such a thing!

Tears

In those early years, the only time I ever saw either Gran or Grandpa exhibit intense emotion was on the afternoon of August 15, 1945, when I was walking back across the bridge from the store. I had almost reached the road up to the cabin. Gran came running down the road, yelling: "Diane Dear, Joey's coming home. . . he's coming home! President Roosevelt just declared the War is over!"

At five, I did not understand much about the war, though we listened to the news every evening. All I knew was Joe left in a uniform and Gran said it would be dangerous. He said it was hard to eat in the barracks because he had to eat with his left hand wrapped completely around his plate, as the other soldiers, all extremely hungry, took rolls and other food off each other's plates.

I liked it better at the cabin. Gran mopped the floor every day with a big rag mop and pail. She always hummed while she mopped or cooked. She had a lovely hum. I learned to dry dishes. I felt like an advanced executive with a very important position. All morning Gran did chores and cooked for our noon dinner. (We had dinner at noon and supper at night.) Gran laid out pink and blue macaroni circles for me to make necklaces or she let me "help" bake by making round balls out of left over uncooked pie dough (after I ate some).

Each night after supper, Grandpa ensconced himself in his big oak rocker and peeled an apple all the way around with his pocket knife, maintaining only one long apple peel. He would slice up the apple and give any children, gathered around the floor at his feet, each a slice. Then he would open up his hand-hewn violin case (that he had made himself as a child) and pull out his antique Paganini Violin. He would play for about a half an hour; sometimes singing along with it. I was fascinated. An almost nightly ritual.

I remember that 7th birthday, on August 10, 1948, before the sad ending with which I began my story. For a birthday party, Gran had invited Sylvia from the grotto of cabins across the highway, Joe Alcorn's nephew, Marianne Pope (our school bus driver's daughter) and a couple others to come for lunch, and gingerbread. They all brought wrapped packages. Halfway through the party, one of the children asked me: "Which present do you like the best?" I responded that I liked the white toy kitten, Sylvia's book,'" then something else and another something else and last, the pink, white, and blue panties that Marianne had given me! Gran was mortified. I was immediately rushed from the party into the kitchen and scolded - first of all, for answering the question. Secondly, for listing Marianne's gift last, as they were a poor family. It was a great sacrifice for her mother to buy me such a lovely Birthday gift! I was marched back to the party with huge apologies to Marianne, explaining how much I loved the color of her gift of blue and pink underpants and how glad I was she could come to the party.

Gran sent Marianne home with all the left over party food and gingerbread, along with a very heavy heart.

The next morning after the breakfast dishes were done Gran went to a lot of trouble to wrap my long hair up in damp rags, which made beautiful long curls when the rags dried.

Life at Rimrock was idyllic for a small child. In my first seven years, I had not a care in the world. I had all the love and nurturing humanly possible by two Grandparents who were educated, affluent, stable, professional, spiritual, talented kind and gentle folks. I thought Gran and Grandpa meant Mommy and Daddy. The other children called their parents Mommy and Daddy. I thought that was what Grandparents were. I loved my home and my family, but it was ripped away from me on my 7th birthday.

William the Conqueror, (1028 – 1087), first Norman King of England; multiple great grandfather of dee McQuesten and Morgan Dowe Davidson; distant cousins of Princess Diana of Wales, also great great granddaughter of William many times over.

Mrs. Wyseman Clagett (1760); great-great aunt of George Dowe McQuesten and dee McQuesten; oil portrait hangs in the Brooklyn Museum Collection of Early American Aristocracy; a Joseph Blackburn painting.

The LaPlante Brothers in San Francisco; Grandfather
Joseph LaPlante bottom right 1863

G. Dowe McQuesten and dee McQuesten's great-great grandfather,
Matthew Thornton, Physician, one of three New Hampshire men
who signed the Declaration of Independence July 4, 1776

Joseph LaPlante, dee McQuesten's great-grandfather;
Puyallup City Clerk (title of town Mayor) 1895

Emma Lundberg, Great Grandmother of dee McQuesten;
wife of Joseph LaPlante; Mother of Maybelle LaPlante
McQuesten, dee's adoptive Mother 1891

1906 Stadium High School in Tacoma, Washington, was converted from a Hotel to a High School. Grandfather G. Dowe McQuesten Christened it on Opening Day with a bottle of champagne, as he was the Director of State Institutions.

Aunt Mary LaPlante Biss, Joseph LaPlante's sister and husband, Charlie Biss, moved from San Francisco to Puyallup to live with Joseph and raise his tiny daughter, Maybelle LaPlante, after her Mother, Emma Lundberg, died of Pneumonia in 1896

Maybelle LaPlante — Age 5 1898

Maybelle LaPlante – Age 16 1909

G. DOWE McQUESTEN

PIERCE COUNTY

House, 1911. Politics, Republican
Born, New Hampshire. Age, 39. Occupation, Lawyer

Here's G. Dowe McQuesten, the sedulous chairman of the Committee on Education and the gallant sponsor of H. B. No. 9. To establish a retirement fund for pensioning teachers, school clerks and others and repealing conflicting laws.—Emergency.

Mr. McQuesten was interested in all educational measures and was very popular with the educators, see cartoon for particulars. He also introduced a bill providing for the development of coal deposits on State Lands.

G. Dowe McQuesten sponsored the first Bill in the Washington State Legislature to provide retirement funds for teachers

G. Dowe McQuesten in Washington State Senate 1921

News of Engagement.

Of special interest in Tacoma is the announcement made last evening in Puyallup of the engagement of Miss Mabel La-Plante to G. Dowe McQuesten. A pre-nuptial "shower" given by the Misses Norman made the interesting news known, surprising friends both in Puyallup and Tacoma, where both families are very well known.

The wedding will take place early in September. Miss LaPlante is a graduate nurse of the Tacoma General hospital. She lately has been assistant in the offices of Dr. W. W. Pascoe. Her father is Joe LaPlante, city clerk of Puyallup for many years. Tacoma guests at the announcement party were Mrs. William Moore, Miss Anita Mossman, Miss Alcora Burke, Miss Florence Burgin, Miss Judith Ahlberg and Miss Elizabeth Turner.

Grandparents' Engagement Announcement in Tacoma News Tribune 1919

LA PLANTE-McQUESTEN WEDDING

A wedding of interest in Tacoma and Puyallup was solemnized Monday morning at 7 o'clock when Miss Mabel LaPlante, daughter of Joseph L. La Plante became the bride of G. Dowe McQuesten. The ceremony was performed by Rev. J. A. Williams, pastor of the First Christian church at the home of the bride. Only immediate relatives of the bride and groom were present.

The bride was unusually attractive in a traveling suit of midnight blue with hat to match. She was attended by Miss Florence McQuesten, sister of the groom.

Miss LaPlante is a graduate of the Puyallup High school and a graduate nurse, having received her training at the Tacoma General Hospital.

Mr. McQuesten is a prominent Tacoma attorney and was for three years a member of the State Board of Control. He was also a member of the state legislature. After November 1, Mr. and Mrs. McQuesten will make their home in Tacoma.

Newspaper Wedding Announcement — September 2, 1919

Maybelle LaPlante's Wedding Day; September 1, 1919

MISS LAPLANT BRIDE OF
TACOMA ATTORNEY

Miss Mabel LaPlante, charming daughter of Joseph LaPlante, was married Monday, September 1st, to G. Dowe McQuesten of Tacoma. The ceremony was performed at the home of the bride's father in Puyallup, at 7 o'clock in the morning, and the happy couple left for Seattle to take the morning boat for Victoria where they went on a honeymoon trip. Rev. J. A. Williams of Tacoma performed the wedding ceremony.

The bride was attired in a going away suit of blue, with a hat to match, and was attended by Miss Florence McQuesten, sister of the bridegroom. Only immediate relatives were present.

The bride is a popular member of the younger set in Puyallup, and was a graduate of the Puyallup high school. She was also graduated a year ago from the Nurses' Training school in the Tacoma General Hospital, and during the past few months she has been assisting in Dr. Pascoe's office in Tacoma.

Mr. McQuesten was a member of the State Board of Control for three years under Governor Ernest Lister. Prior to his appointment to this position, he was a prominent attorney of Tacoma. The couple will establish their home in Tacoma about November 1st, and Mr. McQuesten will again open offices for the practice of law.

A second newspaper announcement September 2, 1919

*Maybelle LaPlante McQuesten's first-born child;
Rosemary McQuesten, Tieton Drive 1921*

Porte Co-Chere led to front terrace, Tieton Drive 1921

Iron Doorstop, Tieton Drive 1921

JOSEPH WINGATE McQUESTEN
Youngest page (12 years) of the 1939 Washington State Legislature.

Joey McQuesten, brother of dee McQuesten 1939

dee McQuesten – First Purse, Tieton Drive 1943

Gran McQuesten taught dee to tie her shoes
behind the Kitchen steps; Tieton Drive 1944

dee McQuesten's First Grade Class; Naches, Washington 1947...
dee 3rd row up from bottom; 3rd in from right side

*Ready for a Gunnysack Race at a Grange
Picnic in Yakima, Washington 1948*

Gran McQuesten on G. Dowe's 90th Birthday;
Sunnyside, Washington 1961

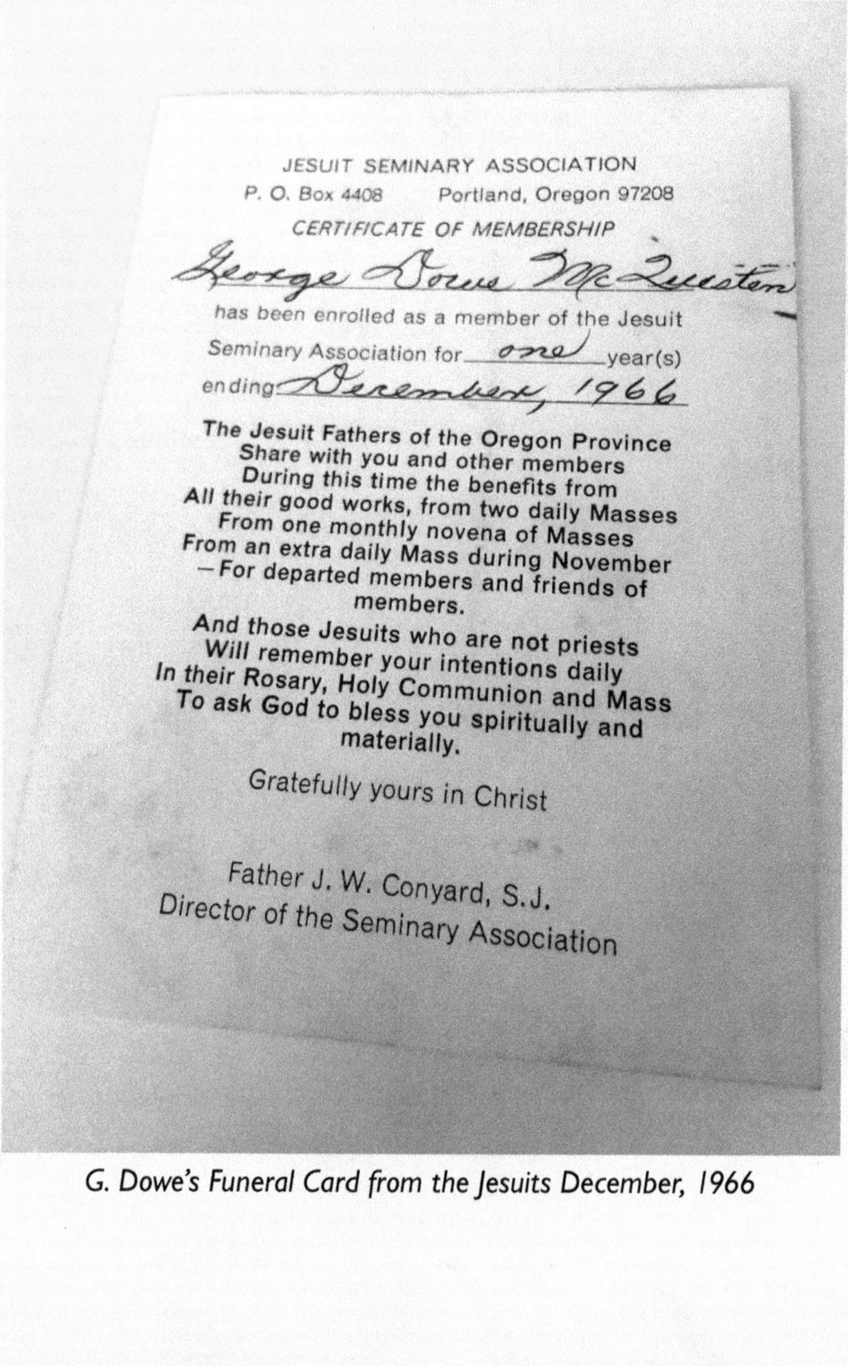

JESUIT SEMINARY ASSOCIATION

P. O. Box 4408   Portland, Oregon 97208

CERTIFICATE OF MEMBERSHIP

George Dowe McQuisten

has been enrolled as a member of the Jesuit

Seminary Association for ___*one*___ year(s)

ending *December, 1966*

The Jesuit Fathers of the Oregon Province
Share with you and other members
During this time the benefits from
All their good works, from two daily Masses
From one monthly novena of Masses
From an extra daily Mass during November
— For departed members and friends of
members.

And those Jesuits who are not priests
Will remember your intentions daily
In their Rosary, Holy Communion and Mass
To ask God to bless you spiritually and
materially.

Gratefully yours in Christ

Father J. W. Conyard, S.J.
Director of the Seminary Association

G. Dowe's Funeral Card from the Jesuits December, 1966

dee McQuesten and Gran on Gran McQuesten's 80th Birthday. dee and sister Emily took Gran home to visit Tieton Drive family home....1973

Morgan Dowe Davidson visited Tieton Drive
Home 48 years later...1989

CHAPTER THREE

Life Far Away from Home

Soon after I was torn from Rimrock, my newly discovered mother took me up the hill to the Magnolia Elementary School on 28th Avenue West. She registered me for 2nd grade and told the lady in the office my name was Diane Spirk. I said, "No," that wasn't my name." My mother said I had to use my step-father's name. I didn't like his name and didn't like him. It was 1948. I was 7.

I began school with a very heavy heart; I thought I was going to Naches Elementary for 2nd grade this year. I was a shy little kid, depressed, fearful and overwhelmed. But here I was and I was reeeeeeeally stuck, wondering if I was ever going home? I could run away, but I didn't know how to get back to Rimrock. Why did I have to leave home? What happened? Did I do something bad? Were they afraid I would throw my clothes in the creek again? I liked Naches School. Miss Thiene taught me how to read. I desperately wanted to go back. I wanted to go to school with Joe Pope and Marianne and the Arneson kids from the Ranger Station. I wanted to roller skate on the tennis court, ride my stilts around the cabin's grotto, ride the school bus with Joe Pope on Halloween and bring all the kids to our cabin where Gran would have the huge caramel popcorn balls for us. I wanted to prowl through the woods with Grandpa and load the trunk with firewood for the winter, take the cardboard box, string and a piece of cheese that Gran gave me to catch chipmunks on the front porch. They said they were going on vacation. Did that mean going away forever?

Soon the letters began to arrive from Gran and Grandpa, twice a week, faithfully, telling me they were home from their vacation and would pick me up on June 16th at the bottom of the school steps. They loved me and missed me and couldn't wait until I could come home for the summer. They were waiting for me.

Still, the letters didn't cover the intense pain from hours of being trapped in Seattle. I had seen on TV that people could kill themselves by simply taking a lot of pills. My mother had buckets of pain and Valium pills. Almost nightly, when they were out partying, I opened her medicine cabinet and counted how many pills she had. I knew I could do it; she had hundreds of pills.

Thank God even my small child's mind thought about Gran and Grandpa. They would be so disappointed if I didn't come home for the summer. I was sure that would make them cry again and the mere thought of making them sad held me back, time after time, after time, as I poked through the medicine cabinet, counting the pills I never took.

Gran, worried already that I was skinny, tried to get me to tell her what they fed me for dinner. I never told her dinner was not a priority in this house. Sometimes I ate bread when my folks were out partying, but I was scolded for that, too; apparently they counted the slices.

Every summer, during those years Gran would say: "Diane dear, I know your mother is mean to you, and I am sorry. I must have done something dreadfully wrong in raising her. I just don't know what I did. Joe and Emma are not mean, but something went wrong with Rosemary. Gran went to her grave blaming herself for my having a mean mother.

I muddled through each school year – went home for the summer – muddled through another year and eventually, finally, after a very, very long wait, arrived at my 18th birthday.

Let me fill in some of that time with stories I remember, some fun, some difficult, all part of very, very trying years in this young girl's life.

When I was 10, I had to have my tonsils and adenoids removed. My folks dropped me off at Doctors' Hospital on Seneca Street in Seattle. They did not return for three days, apparently (no, *obviously*) quite glad to be rid of me. The nurses and doctors kept popping into my hospital room, saying, "Where are your parents?", day after day, shaking their heads. The Saturday after I got home from the hospital I was alone as usual. Ann Webb, a neighbor friend, came over. We played Monopoly all afternoon. And Sunday the same. Ann didn't seem to notice how dirty the house was. We stayed in my small room, which I kept clean.

On Monday morning, my mother was anxious to get me out of the house. She cooked scrambled eggs and tomato juice. OUCH! The acid in the tomato juice really burned my throat. She didn't care. I begged her not to make me drink it. She said I had to sit there until it was gone, even if I had to sit there all day. It took two hours to finish the juice. My mother wrote a note to my teacher saying: "deedee is late today because she refused to eat her breakfast." Since neither my birth mother nor my step-father wanted me, as I was again inconvenient, it would have been easy to return me to my Grandparents. However, as much as my birth mother hated her parents (and everyone else), her power play was to force me to live with her, cutting deeply into my Grandparents' hearts.

I never did confide in Gran the state of our living conditions, as I knew she would be very upset and sick with worry. My sister, Em, informed me that my Grandparents wanted my birth mother to be happy in a marriage to a stable man. They thought Scotty would create a good home life for her. Gran always believed she did something wrong in raising Rosemary, but didn't know what that had been. She went to her grave (the Sunday before Morgan was born) believing she was somehow responsible for Rosemary being so mean. That didn't make any sense, since she and Grandpa were so loving with Joe, Em and I.

I did find out, years after Rosemary died, through a series of tests I took, that she was ADD. The psychiatrist who administered the test told me when not treated, it often turns to schizophrenia or paranoia or both.

Moving on, when I was 8 or 9, I joined Lynda Poeppel and Valerie Dent's Brownie Troop. I loved going to their homes every Tuesday. Their homes were clean and their mothers were warm and friendly. Kristine Rouse's father, Detective Charlie Rouse, drove us home in his SPD squad car. That was cool beyond belief. He was jolly; I thought Kristine was reeeeeeally lucky to have such a nice dad.

In third grade, I had a crush on one of my classmates, Bill Burley. One afternoon I walked home with him after school. He and Pete Jobs lived next to a tennis court. He asked me to wait on the court bench while he dashed in and changed his clothes. He came out with Pete and a tennis racket. I watched my first tennis game. I had never seen anyone play tennis, even though Monty Hadzer had a court on the caretaker's grounds at Rimrock. Simultaneously fascinated and thrilled, I watched for at least two hours, stopping only when my stepfather came driving by, saw me and angrily drove me home. Another whooppin!

Just days later, I discovered my mother had an old racket left over from her days on the Rimrock court. Pay dirt!!! I found out that Kate Metheney, a year ahead me in school, liked to play. She agreed to teach me. We began playing for hours on the two courts behind the Magnolia Theater on 34th Avenue (now a fire station); I thought tennis the greatest sport on earth. I still do!

New "Ir-Responsibilities"

I discovered myself burdened with two new responsibilities. My stepfather, a Lt. Commander in the Naval Reserve, traveled frequently, to Pensacola, San Diego and San Francisco. While he was gone, my mother had a series of mini-affairs with husbands in the neighborhood. It became my unpleasant task to answer the phone and lie to their wives, denying their husbands were at our house. Sometimes, I had to answer the door when wives arrived, demanding to see their husbands, telling them their husbands were not at our house, saying my birth mother was not home!

That was not half as embarrassing, however, as my birth mother's attempts to hook up with the middle school and high school boys in my class!

My birth mother figured out a new ruse: At the Pier 91 Naval Officers' Club she became acquainted with Captain Salonga, Chief of Staff of the Philippine Navy, stationed in Seattle for a year or so. It was convenient for him to come to the house during the day when Scotty worked as a Quality Control Engineer at Boeing. There was, however, a significant problem: Captain Salonga wore a very heavy mens' cologne. When my stepfather arrived home after work and smelled the distinctly pungent odor, more fighting and screaming ensued.

My birth mother insisted that I go on double dates with her, Captain Salonga and his young 20-year-old Attache. Strangest thing ever; double-dating with my married birth mother!!!

Escapes

Aside from tennis, my escape in those days was babysitting, a service I offered for .25 cents an hour. In addition to caring for the children, I washed the dinner dishes, cleaned the kitchen and mopped the floor. In demand, this suited me well, as I loved children and it got me out of a dreadful house.

I also truly loved ice skating. On Saturdays, I took the bus down to the Civic Ice Arena, in what is now the Pacific Northwest Ballet facility (named the Marion Oliver McCaw Hall). Robin Kettenring, Patty Reed and I took lessons from Carol Mithun in dancing on ice and figures. I relished skating really fast and dancing, particularly the Dutch Waltz. The overhead music inspired me. I bought a pair of hand-made Oberhammer white leather skates with my baby-sitting money. I was very proud of those skates. Sometimes after school Patty's Mom, Clara, drove us out to the Ballard Ice Arena for "Patch" – the practice of figure skating.

When I was in junior high school, the predominant saving grace was Donald Libby, orchestra leader and music teacher. One day, there was a school-wide announcement that anyone who would like to play in the school orchestra should report to the Cafeteria at 1:00. If you did not play an instrument, Mr. Libby would help you learn one. That sounded like great fun to me. I reported in. Jeanne Ragan already knew how to play the cello brilliantly. Julie

Bates already played the flute. Paul Barrett played the clarinet and Alan Walker was a talented drummer. (Alan planned to go to med school, become a surgeon; subsequently play classical music in his operating rooms.) Mr. Libby asked me what instrument I would like to learn. I had no idea. I loved the piano, but my mother said we couldn't afford one; I was at a loss as to what other instrument I should learn. He suggested I might do well on the viola – 2" longer than a violin and an octave lower. He had a school viola I could use. That seemed fine to me. Mr. Libby taught us to read music, spending individual time with each student. When he had taught me all he could, he sent me to a private teacher for about 6 months. My step-father begrudgingly paid. I practiced hard, but it didn't come naturally. I was thrilled playing in the orchestra, but it was such difficult time-consuming work I did not pursue it in high school.

(Many years later, in the early 80's, Bob Watt, chairing the Board at the Seattle Symphony, heard I formerly played viola, asked me to audition for a viola vacancy. He had no idea what he was asking. I was flattered, knowing that was far above my pay grade! I didn't audition.)

In both Magnolia Elementary and Catherine Blaine we had field trips downtown to the Orpheum Theater to see the Seattle Symphony. The Conductor, Stanley Chapple, introduced one instrument at a time, explaining the history of the instrument and how each fit in with the orchestra. I was mesmerized; playing in an actual orchestra at Catherine Blaine Orchestra was thrilling.

Mr. Libby himself played the trumpet in Jackie Souder's band at night. I can still hear him playing "It's Cherry Pink and Apple Blossom White."

One day, in Spring, 1957, there was another school-wide announcement that the Magnolia Branch Library was hiring a new person. I went down to McGraw Street and applied. They hired me to be a Page; shelving books after school. I loved to read. I stopped every few minutes to look through a book, perhaps to read a few passages. I took home armloads of books to read, sometimes under the covers at night with a flashlight. Miss Hansmann, the Branch Librarian, spoke to me about reading when I should be working, shelving books, not devouring them. I tried to discipline myself, occasionally lapsing, forcing Miss Hansmann to speak to me again. After about three months, she tactfully explained that the City of Seattle was cutting her budget and she could no longer afford to pay me, softening the blow of being fired from my first job. That was okay. I still joined the Summer Reading Club and took stacks of books home to Gran's each summer and earned Certificates each summer's end for reading tons of books.

My birth mother had a feisty manx cat, Bobby, who each day used the laundry trays as a litter box. It was my job to clean out the trays every day after school. From the time I was 8, in 1949, I was given a .25 cent allowance to feed the cat, clean his dishes, do all the ironing for the whole family and weed the garden beds. For any mistake, they deducted 5 cents off my allowance.

Walking distance from home, The Magnolia Theater on 34th had Saturday matinees – Roy Rogers, Trigger and Tonto; Hopalong Cassidy and the like. For 20 cents you could see the movie. 5 cents more would buy a package of candy or a bag of popcorn. I rarely got my whole allowance, as I would forget one of my stepfather's long sleeved white office shirts that needed to be starched and ironed or neglected washing one cat dish, I never got the popcorn. If I made two mistakes, there would be no movie.

The End Table Tale

One summer afternoon, while I was home, in Yakima, Joey came by the house to tell Grandpa that he had just rented a space in a Sunnyside office building to hang his CPA shingle. He had been practicing in Yakima for years for the Dewey Frame CPA firm, but decided to change his location.

Grandpa immediately drove the 30-minute distance to Sunnyside, located the owner of the building and wrote him a check for the entire building. He brought the Deed and Title home, and endorsed it over to Joey, with the same advice he gave all of us over the years:

1. "Now then, you own the building. You rent or lease out the spaces yourself.
2. Never pay anyone rent.
3. Never lease from anyone.
4. Never buy or borrow on credit.
5. Never use a credit card of any type
6. Never pay interest.
7. Never take out a loan; even a mortgage. Cash only"

While Gran was happy to see Grandpa generously gift this building to Joey, she had asked for a small mahogany end table for the living to use at the end of the sofa. Grandpa was not interested in spending money on such nonsense!

One night, months later, when I was back in middle school in Seattle, we got a call from Joey that Gran was missing! The whole family was terrified, as there were no clues as to her whereabouts.

Grandpa, one of the more affluent citizens in Yakima, at first, feared she had been kidnapped. But there were no requests for ransom.

Three terrifying days went by. Finally a very relieved Joey called to tell us what had happened.

Grandpa had found the mahogany end table Gran had asked for up-ended in the hall coat closet. He realized Gran, unable to bear the thought of G. Dowe yelling at her, must be staying with her best friend, Jesse Hedges, only a few blocks away, up on Nob Hill Avenue. Grandpa called Jesse, saying: "You can tell Mabel I found the end table. She can come home now because she can keep it!"

With hindsight, we all wondered what Grandpa had been eating for 3 days, since Gran had cooked three meals a day for him for many, many decades! He was too much of a tight Scot for restaurants. We never knew the answer to that question, but he did appear to be a little thinner!

High School Trauma

As I got older, I did not escape trauma at Queen Anne High School. For the first day of my Senior Year, I had worked to save some babysitting money to buy some new school clothes. Elected an "alternative" to the Fashion Board at Bests' Apparel, I bought a pale blue Evan Picone wool skirt and matching sweater of lambs wool. I was quite proud of my new outfit.

But by 9:00 a.m. that first day, I was overcome with menstrual pain. This had happened many times before. My doctor had tried a variety of pain medications. The only thing that helped even slightly, was morphine, which made me quite ill; nauseous. There was no good answer. That first morning, I passed out in the girls bathroom on the first floor. The next thing I knew, Jim Gibson and my friend, Barbara Steen, were carrying me out on a gurney to Barb's car. They took me home and put me to bed. Added to the embarrassment at the scene I had caused, when Barb saw how dirty our house – all the table tops covered with ashes, cigarette butts, empty beer and Galiano bottles – she exclaimed: "Oh Diane, I had no idea!" I will never forget the tone of shock in her voice. So much for my long-awaited first day of Senior Year!

There were other high school traumas. Pete Meier, whose uncle was Stan Sayers of Seattle hydroplane "Slo Mo" fame, after whom the pits are still named, invited me to visit the pit and see his uncle's hydroplane. My birth mother, an extremely prejudiced and hypo-critical atheist, wouldn't let me go. She suspected Pete was Jewish.

Peter Wickstrand, and Bill Weisfield had been my shop partners back in Mr Billodue's Shop Class at Catherine Blaine. When we made plastic hearts with a color inside, Pete made one with red coloring and gave it to Nancy Johanson, who sat on his right side. Prior to that, Peter had invited me to a house party at his parents' home. But I was not allowed that, either, because my birth mother had discovered Peter Wickstrand's family was Catholic. This had been my chance to socialize and have some fun with my peers.

I didn't notice that Bill gave his to anyone. The heart I made had blue inside. I still have it on a thin silver chain.

I did manage one contact with a religious/spiritual friend, Bill Weisfield, who was my friend in school, too. His family was Jewish. One Friday I attended a beautiful service with Bill and his parents at Temple de Hirsch, unbeknownst to my strange birth mother. It was a stunning service inside a Temple on Capitol Hill. I had never seen anything like it. It was quite like watching a movie. Very moving; very reverent. I didn't understand the Hebrew, but I loved the pageantry of it. It left a lifetime impression on me, always wish I could return for another Sabbath Service.

Regarding religion, Gran wrote regularly that I should find a church to attend every Sunday. Magnolia Lutheran Church had several of my classmates in their Sunday School class, so I asked if I could go. My folks said I could, but, as they disapproved, I would have to walk. It was over a mile and freezing in the rain, but even in winter, I walked to and fro every Sunday. I was too shy to ask if I might ride with someone else. So I walked and I walked and I walked. Every Saturday morning for classes and every Sunday morning for church and choir. As a choir member, I practiced diligently for the Christmas concert. My folks were out partying the night of the concert, however; they did not have time to take me so I missed it. I was crushed.

In high school, my friends began attending the Church of the Ascension Episcopal Church at the opposite/north end of Magnolia Village. I enjoyed it a lot, even teaching Sunday school my junior year. Sue Linforth and Ann Rystogi's parents regularly drove me one way/home/ after Sunday morning services. It was a long, cold walk in the winter rain, so I was grateful. Don Miller, our Youth Pastor, was a terrific mentor to all of us. I was eventually Confirmed and joined the Episcopal Church, where I remained until 1977 when I became Catholic.

dee McQuesten and John Ruud; Lincoln Junior Prom.....1957

CHAPTER FOUR

Free at Last, Free at Last

Graduating from high school, I was quite immature, unsure of myself, wanting to belong, eager to get away from the terrible home that inflicted such continuous pain 10 months a year from age 7 to 18. Eleven long years.

My 18th Birthday arrived in the middle of Rush Week at the University of Washington. Free at last! I chose a sorority house, and moved in from the dorm. On my first week there my birth mother called – from California. She had moved without any notice to anyone. She had arranged her move for the day after I moved to the U.W. campus. Bekins Van and Storage came early the next morning. They quickly packed, moved her totally in one day; furniture, household goods and clothes. She moved to California.

My stepfather arrived home from work that night to a note on the floor in a *completely* empty house. There were no towels, no silverware, no plates, no furniture, nothing! Two weeks later he showed up at my sorority, asking my help to track her down. I didn't have a clue. All she said when she called me what that she was in California. Scotty had to buy all new furniture! Though confused because it happened so suddenly, I was frankly relieved.

When I went through Rush, in 1959, I blundered terribly. I chose a sorority because there was one girl in the house whom I liked very much from my Queen Anne High School. Most of my Pledge Class from the same high school, Roosevelt, were already friends. They were pretentious, social wanna-be's. The sorority had a zillion senseless rules and regs; I was miserable. We could not walk into our first floor lobby unless we were wearing a girdle. They gave us a list of three fraternities and three fraternities only, we were encouraged to date exclusively. Most of my high school friends were "Independents," either living in the dorms or commuting from home. We were not allowed to socialize with Independents, as it was bad for the "house image". Friends in other sororities had none of these restrictions. Early on, I was "caught" having coffee with an Independent girlfriend from my class at Queen Anne in the HUB. I was grounded for two weeks.

I went to the Dean of Women asking to be transferred to the Dorms. I hated sorority living. I wanted nothing to do with any of this. The Dean called my birth-mother, in California, who had basically abandoned me again, really had nothing to do with my college education for which my grandparents were paying; she insisted I stay in the sorority house, refusing to allow me to transfer to the dorms. Having joined the wrong house, I was trapped! After my freshman year, I walked out of the house with a huge sigh of relief, never to step inside again.

I experienced another problem that first year. These people at the University seemed not to realize my vast academic abilities. We had no homework at Queen Anne that could not be accomplished in Study Hall. My first class that first quarter at the U.W. was World History 110 in Architecture Hall. 610 of us. I sat so high up the aisle that I couldn't possibly tell what Professor Giovanni Costigan looked like if I saw him on the street! Costigan, a renowned scholar and revered teacher, announced that for every hour we spent in lecture, we were to spend 2 outside of class studying. But Professor Costigan didn't know that I had graduated from Queen Anne with excellent grades and didn't need to do homework. Other students may need such rigor, but not I, perhaps smarter than the other 609!

I walked out on more than just sorority living. Miserable, I began skipping classes, papers and exams. Dean Riley called me in after my second quarter to say if my grades didn't improve, he would have to expel me. I really didn't care. Wretchedly unhappy, I didn't want to be there, anyway. Also, strangely, though I had never been part of the popular crowd in high school, now, suddenly I was getting 20 to 30 calls a week for fraternity parties and coffee dates – three to five times calls than anyone else in the sorority. Un-explainable. I had met a few people in classes and a few people at the keg parties the sorority had set up, but could scarcely imagine all these phone calls. I had always thought I was a wallflower. When, occasionally I attended the Queen Anne PTA dances, rarely did anyone ever ask me to dance. Why the sudden interest in me? I am still unsure what brought about this change.!

Still, I didn't want to be in the sorority, nor did I need to do all that studying; Dean Riley could threaten all he wanted. At the end of spring quarter, Mrs. Williams, our Housemother, told me that Dean Riley wanted to see me. I walked across campus to his office in the Ad Building. He said, almost with a smile: "My dear, you have distinguished yourself in the annals of the University of Washington. You have accumulated the lowest GPA of any student we have had thus far – a .0213 GPA. Now you really are expelled."

At the time, I didn't care as much as my disappointed sorority sisters whose accumulative house grade-point I had demolished. Our house was consistently first or second in the campus Greek system for our grade point average. The only house we competed with was the Kappa house. No one else seemed to come near the gpa we garnered, for some odd reason. At least that was for the three quarters I lived on campus.

The week school let out, I went directly to the Boeing Employment Office and applied for work. They hired me on the spot. After a year of riding a typewriter, I began to think there was something to this education business after all. Typing material I didn't understand for eight hours every day was terminally boring! I was working in the Quality Control Building on West Marginal Way, 7 a.m. to 3 p.m., typing drafted drawings of airplane parts.

I went back to campus and talked to Dean Riley. Amazingly, he offered: "I'll tell you what I'll do: you can come back at night and take a 5-hour course Tuesdays and Thursdays from 7:00-9:30 or 10:00. If you get an A or a B, come back and see me. I'll authorize you to return for one more quarter and take another 5-hour class."

Eventually, despite myriad changes over the years, I did that, going to night classes for 6 years, working in Eddie Carlson's, the President's Office, at Westin Hotels during the day as his Travel Agent Liaison, airline scheduler for the company's 42 execs, and Secretary to the company's General Sales Manager, while taking classes at night.

CHAPTER FIVE

A Less than Ideal Marriage

Simultaneously, at 20 years old, without nearly enough reflection, I married my freshman sweetheart, (whom I will call) Terry. December 16, 1961.

Looking back, I know I had a deep desire for a home, a family, a place to belong, be nourished, be at peace. From age 7 to 18, for 10 months a year, I had lived with chaos, being constantly denigrated, with both physical and psychological abuse. Somewhere deep inside I knew the early home I had with Gran and Grandpa was possible. I wanted to be part of such a home, such a family. It was not to be . . . at least, not yet.

The calamities surrounding our wedding day might have provided warnings this relationship was doomed….a foreboding.

On December 15, 1961, Terry's mother put on a rehearsal dinner at their home in Blue Ridge. My family was not invited. Grand and Grandpa were not invited. It was, however, beautifully done in red and white. Margaret, Terry's mother, was artistically talented. However, long before, during and after the dinner, my future mother-in-law, insultingly announced to anyone and everyone the totally unfounded assertion that we were getting married because I was pregnant!

We were married at the Episcopal Church of the Ascension in Magnolia. Things kept going wrong. Gran, after begging me and pleading tearfully to wait until I finished college to get married, designed and stitched a beautiful white satin gown for me. It was the most beautiful wedding gown I had ever seen! The day of the wedding, about 7:30, I realized no one was picking me up to get to the church. I called my fiance, Terry, who said he didn't have time. In addition, his mother wouldn't let him use one of the family cars. If he collected me from my little Magnolia apartment, he would be late to the church! I called church, but there was no answer. It was snowing out. I could not get a cab. Finally, at 7:45, Judy Weisfield called from a pay phone. She and Bill had driven up from Beaverton for the wedding. She wondered if I needed anything! They picked me up. I made it to the church just in time; well, almost - just five minutes late.

Before I arrived, I later discovered, Barb Steen, a bridesmaid, was distraught; she had used the Ladies' room and the two long red satin sashes at the end of her big bow on the back of her bridesmaid dress had fallen in the toilet! Always ingenious, she found a pair of the church's gardener shears to cut off the soaked sashes – a very ragged, unseemly cut, but what was left of the bow was dry!

After the reception, no one could locate my suitcase. Gran had sewn a beautiful blue two-piece going-away outfit. Finally, after locating my belongings, Terry was still searching for his missing rented tux. His groomsman, Steve Duzan, discovered it, all but destroyed, outside in the snow, accidentally dropped on the way to the car. We had intended to use Terry's parents' white Cadillac as our getaway car, but when we went to get in, we found it with a flat tire.

No one wanted to change the tire in the snow, understandably.

Most difficult of all that fateful wedding day, neither Terry nor I knew anything about sex, except for two per-marital counseling sessions with Cannon Poland H. Miller, my Pastor at Ascension. When we found sex difficult, I recalled the book he had given us had a suggestion that, if sex was stressful, use a lubricant; it suggested Vaseline. We didn't have any Vaseline, so I used Mentholatum. **OUCH!!!** The internal burning sensation lasted several days.

The final mishap happened as we stayed overnight in a hotel by Sea-Tac Airport. When I went to put my luggage in the car, my jewelry case was missing. I returned to an empty hotel room. We located the manager, who searched widely, finally locating it in a maid's locker where it was hidden! Another disaster averted!

From day one in our marriage, I was financially responsible for putting Terry through day school at the U.W. His parents, Margaret and John, asked me to promise to finance Terry through his last three years of college; tuition, books, fees, living expenses, etc. He had a small partial tennis scholarship for the first couple of years, but no longer. They said since Terry was married, they felt they had no financial responsibility to see that he finished his Undergraduate Degree at the U.W. I paid the rest of his school expenses and our living costs for the next three years with what I earned in Mr. Carlson's office at the Westin Executive Office on the 12th Floor of the Olympic Hotel.

We lived those first three years mostly on 55th N.E. in one of Bob Schloredt's apartment houses. Bobby was the Husky's fabled one-eyed quarterback; we loved him, as a true gentleman and good soul. For a reduction in rent, it was my responsibility to keep the apartment compound's laundry room clean. For convenience we later moved up to 15th avenue, just a block from campus.

Against my will, I turned all of my paychecks over to Terry to manage, who was miserly, at best. He begrudgingly gave me .25 cents lunch money each morning to buy a "cup" of soup in the Olympic Hotel Grill – never a bowl, costing .75 cents. There was, however, a penny tax on a quarter in those days. I didn't have the penny. Daily I borrowed a penny from my office friend, Fran Vitulli Lindquist. A great deal of the money I was earning went to pay initiation and dues at the Seattle Golf Club, solely for Terry's benefit, as I had very little time to golf! However, all day Saturdays and Sundays, he played golf with his father, John, while I was home studying, cleaning house, cooking and planning meals for the week, in addition to handling all the yard work. **What** was I thinking?

Terry, while extremely bright, could be arrogant. I recall one sunny summer Saturday prior to our marriage, we ventured up to Paradise/Mount Rainier with my Tacoma roommate, Ann Cook, (Cookie) and her boyfriend, Mike. My job was to make potato salad, which I did, in my humble opinion, quite well. We opened our picnic baskets on a Paradise lawn table and benches. Halfway through lunch, Terry said, "Where are the pickles? Potato salad is supposed to have pickles in it!" Exasperated for once, I stood up, lifted the bowl of salad and dumped approximately 5 pounds of potato salad on Terry's arrogant head.

Since Terry refused to help me, financially, finish my undergraduate degree, Gran always sent me a check for my books each quarter. Five years into our marriage, my grandparents purchased and furnished a home for us in the Seattle Green Arbor neighborhood, two blocks east of Blue Ridge, where Terry's family resided.

As far as Terry was concerned, women didn't need degrees. Why waste my time when I should be generating an income. The irony never seemed to occur to him of talking about my wasting money when we were living in a home provided by my family! Terry became employed by the world's largest public accounting house; soon to be their youngest Managing Partner.

An Anti-Social Social Life

We did have a modicum of a social life; for me, squeezed in between my working multiple part-time jobs simultaneously and U.W. classes.

However, that social life was often unpleasant and demeaning. I remember bitterly one specific sailing dinner party on a Sunday afternoon at my friend Marion Martin's parents' home. Marion headed the Design Department for Naramore, Bain, Brady, & Johansen. Her parents' beautiful sailboat was moored at their home on Mercer Island. After a glorious 45-minute sail, 40 of us went into the Martins' home for supper. Gary Little, Marion's date, announced this was a "pre-engagement" party. Prior to seating in the dining room, we were gathered around having a glass of wine and hors d'oeuvres. Five of us were collected in a circle at one end of the living room, as Marion was commenting that she felt thrilled and privileged to be the first woman to graduate from Yale University's School of Architecture and Design. Terry, standing next to me, turned, and whispered in my right ear "You are not welcome in this conversation group!"

Humiliated and demeaned, I moved without a word across the room toward other dinner guests. I never had an answer for his hurtful comments, consistently in public social gatherings, sometimes out of hearing range of other guests; sometimes not.

What was wrong with this picture? I had just put Terry through 3 years of college, working multiple part-time jobs to support him, while attending UW night school 2 nights a week – *and* he was living in a very nice home Gran had purchased for us. All Terry had to do was attend his classes and do his homework. No part-time jobs; just cruising along unemcumbered for three years.

There was something here I didn't get. Why was he so mean? There were other young married couples in the room. I didn't see or hear any of the other husbands speak to their wives in that manner. Grandpa never spoke to Gran like that! Aside from arrogance, Terry had a very strong sense of "entitlement".

Terry reminded me too often of my birth mother, perpetually yelling at me, "You're beautiful, but you're DUMB!" I hated that; I didn't want to be beautiful! I wanted to be SMART, like Gran, Grandpa, Emmy and Joey. I am not dumb. Why couldn't Terry see that? Why was I married to him? I felt trapped. I needed to finish my degree. Then go my own way.

I was constantly aware that I had made a promise in church/to God, "For better or for worse." Did that mean anything and everything was okay ? What did that pledge cover? Over and over I wondered "Is this what God wants me to do? Spend my life like this? " My heart felt very heavy and confused – and afraid. I was trapped in a terrible relationship.

I had only seen such personal attacks between my alcoholic screaming "school year" parents. Never ONCE did Grandpa put down Gran or criticize her; not in front of me or anyone in the family - much less in public. I am positive he didn't criticize or demean her in private, either. I would have seen at least a glimmer of it.

I had no response to such behavior, other than to rock back on my heels, in shock. No matter how often it happened, I was always stunned, hurt, saddened, with no response. Just knots in my stomach.

I was pretty thin in those days, more fuel for Terry's fodder. His favorite form of humiliation was to announce, anywhere, at home – or in public: "You don't even need a bra. Why don't you buy yourself a couple of tee-shirts?"

Terry actually struck me only three times. The third was the worst.

I didn't know what would set him off – didn't see it coming.

Out of nowhere, he swung at me with his right fist, smashed me on the left side of my face, eye and ear again, knocking me to the floor clear across the room!

I feared he would end my life if I didn't escape. The rage in his eyes was alarming.

Pulling myself up, I raced to the kitchen, grabbed my keys and purse, tore out the kitchen door and flung myself into the driver's seat of my car. I remember now how cold it was, but I didn't have time to grab a coat. This time he was going to teach me a lesson for good, if he could catch me, and catch me he tried, running across the lawn to the passenger side of my car. The door was locked.

I backed out of the driveway as fast as any human could, racing down the street before he could jump in his car to catch me. I took many twists and turns to avoid him following me.

Again, I had no money – not even the .25 cents Terry gave me each morning for a cup of soup at lunch time (out of my own paycheck) I had nothing but three good jobs!

I did have a checkbook in my purse, to an empty checking account.

As an employee in the Executive Office of Westin Hotels (housed on the 12th Floor of the Olympic Hotel) I could have complementary lodging at any of our hotels.

However, I could not stay at the Olympic, where I had worked for over a decade, my red and bruised face now swelling with my eye turning black and blue, my ear bleeding. I could not go to the Benjamin Franklin (now re-named the Westin), as I knew the whole staff. Where to go without a single penny?

The YWCA on 5th Avenue said they would take a check. (They assumed there was money in my account.) The overnight cost at that time, in 1968, was about $ 18.00, if my memory serves me correctly.

The Registration Woman at the Front Desk was like my afternoon Boss at the Edmond Meany Hotel, concerned about my battered face, asked if I needed help.

Could she help me make a Police Report? Could she send some-one, a social worker, to talk to me? How about medication? Could she give me something to ease the pain in my swollen face so I could sleep?

"No", I replied. "I don't like to take pills." I was soooooo exhaust-ed, I wanted to find a room and sleep. "I'm going to park my car in the Olympic Garage. I'll be right back. I'm so grateful you have a room available." I knew the Olympic would take my check because I had I.D. with me that said I was a 12th Floor employee.

"It will just be one night," I told her. "I need a couple extra blan-kets, as I am very cold; I have no coat to throw over my bed. Thank you, but I don't want to talk with anyone tonight. I'm too tired. I will figure something else out for lodging tomorrow. Thank you for your help and concern. No, I don't need a Police Report. I'll be okay."

I declined her offer of a coat from their Lost and Found.

I felt safe there, at the "Y". Terry would not figure out where I was.

The next morning I called in sick to the office, telling the Office Manager I had severe menstrual cramps. "I might be out for a couple of days, as it is worse than usual this month."

My face wasn't going to look that much better in a couple of days. Maybe I would take a few vacation days for the swelling to go down before I faced the office. Meanwhile, I could attend my classes at UW, not knowing anyone in my classes, including my Professors.

I was in too much physical and emotional pain to think ahead. I desperately wanted to go to sleep and not try to think any longer tonight.

I don't recall what I did the next morning. I had no money to buy breakfast -- anywhere. What I do recall is that I waited out the morning somehow until 2:00; then drove by the house, hoping to find Terry's car gone, so I could go in and get a coat. It was winter. I was freezing.

His car was gone. I hurried in and grabbed my toothbrush, toothpaste, the warm winter coat Gran had given me, and school books, without the faintest idea where I could go with no money.

As I bolted out the front door, Terry drove up.

Terrified, I stood paralyzed on the front lawn, thinking he wouldn't do anything out in the open in front of the neighbors - hopefully.

Instead, and for the third time, he exited his car with a long box of red roses, tied up in a large red satin bow, tears streaming down his face, saying, "Come into the house. I want to talk to you."

Terry was so emotionally wrought, I didn't think he would hit me. He was doubled over in anguish, weeping.

Once inside, he begged me not to leave him, saying how sorry he was and it would never, ever happen again. That was the third time I had seen the tears, been gifted the long stem red roses and heard that it would never happen again.

I knew it would, but my drive to finish college was motivated and intense. Terry begrudgingly gave me enough money out of my paychecks to cover my tuition and fees. Gran was mailing me money for my textbooks; only a little while longer. I could make it. There was nothing in the world I wanted more than my University of Washington Diploma, after 9 long years of working toward that goal.

Time to move on. I graduated in August, left the hotel company and went to work for Seattle Mental Health shortly thereafter, filed for Divorce in April, signed the final documents in October and moved to Massachusetts in March with Mandy Dodd one year later.

Work Related vignettes

My senior year at the University of Washington required day classes and a full schedule. I worked in President Carlson's office downtown, from 8 to 10:30 in the morning, caught a bus to campus at 10:45, attended an 11:30 and 12:30 class and raced as fast as I could over to the Edmond Meany Hotel on 45th in the University District for my afternoon job, which was from 2:00 to 5:00 (General Manager John Ramsey's secretary). Mr. Ramsey was simultaneously also he General Manager of the Crystal Mountain Ski Resort.

An odd thing happened while working for Mr. Ramsey: one afternoon, while I had slipped over to the restroom, someone stole my wallet out of my bottom desk drawer on the hotel's Mezzanine.

Two weeks later, Frederick & Nelson's Billing Office (in downtown Seattle where Nordstrom's is now) called me about something wrong with the signature on a Charge Slip for Purchase. They mailed me a copy of the signature. It wasn't mine. I told them my wallet had been stolen at work. They asked me if I recognized the signature. I didn't. But I had an idea.

It was near Mr. Ramsay's birthday. I bought a large birthday card and marched through the building, asking everyone on every shift sign the card. I asked the head of Personnel for a list of employees. I took a photo of the card and sent it to Frederick's. The head of their "In-House Theft Department" came to the Edmond Meany to see me a month later. They had identified one signature on the card as the handwriting of the thief. He offered me a job to join Frederick & Nelson as an Assistant Detective in his department!

That job didn't interest me; the arrangement I already had with the hotel company allowed me to attend my final UW classes.

After asking several times over some weeks how much was spent on my Frederick & Nelson credit card and what were the purchases, the Theft Department finally relented and told me. A young man had purchased a $ 2.00 dress from Frederick's Bargain Basement for his mother for Mothers' Day. Really? All this fuss over $ 2.00? If a hotel employee had asked me for $ 2.00 to buy his mother a Mothers' Day gift as a favor, I would have GIVEN it to him!!! That sales price, $ 2.00, even in May, 1967, would have to have been the mother of all dress sales!

A stinging memory I have from working for Mr. Ramsay ("Mr." Ramsay and "Mr." Carlson, because the hotel business was quite formal), is one afternoon when I arrived at my desk, Mr. Ramsay, greeted me. After a brief glance, he asked: "Where did you get that shiner?" I thought I had covered up my black eye fairly well with makeup, but he saw through the swelling. I replied, "Terry hit the brakes. I bounced off of the dashboard."

He said, "You didn't get that black eye off a dashboard!" He was extremely upset. He said, "Are you okay? Are you in danger? Is there anything you can tell me or want to talk about? You can trust me." "Can I make a Police Report for you?" Eventually he gave up, as I wouldn't discuss it. I carefully avoided seeing anyone I knew personally for at least ten days. I didn't know anyone in my UW classes, so I didn't have to offer any explanations. This happened on three separate occasions.

My morning job office mates and colleagues in Mr. Carlson's office also inquired about my black eyes, on three different incidents, but each time seemed to accept the fact that this was a dashboard event, or I walked into a door in the middle of the night at home. They were all convinced I was a hopeless klutz. Which was what I wanted them to think.

I managed to fool everyone except Mr. Ramsay. I knew if I told him the truth, he would pressure me to get out of the marriage and do it quickly. I had already made the decision to stay married until I completed my degree at UW. I felt it would be too complicated to get a divorce while I was working three jobs and finishing college. It wasn't doable. My mind was made up. I set my cap and powered on. Only 3 black eyes and a few bruises in 8 years! I could survive this. Now was not the time to try to reconfigure my life.

To survive financially, on top of these two jobs, I added a third part- time job that almost did me in – I became a cashier at Steil & King Mens' Store in the Northgate Mall. I caught the bus from the U district to Northgate at 5:05 p.m. I worked weeknights from 5:30 to 9:30 p.m. Finally, I went home to study 'til the wee hours. In a near miracle, I made it to graduation.

One conversation sustaining me during those years, besides my grand-parents' continual encouragement and reassurance that I was doing the right thing, was an accidental conversation supportive of my education with my Civics Teacher from Queen Anne High School. One morning, while walking across campus, I ran into Mr. John Koruga. He asked me what I was doing. He told me he was proud of me and he wanted me to remember that "every credit I earned was like money in the bank; no one could take that away from me. An education is forever, so keep going; keep stockpiling those credits and you'll make it." I played our brief conversation over and over and over in my head during difficult moments; especially when required to take a math course and 10 hours of science to graduate. UGH!

And then there was my birth mother. She married again, Alexander Karuzin, a rocket scientist at Warner's, I believe a sub-set of Lockheed. Alex was a brilliant, funny, generously spirited and caring soul. They lived in Los Altos. One spring in 1966 they drove to Seattle. They came by my office and took me shopping at John Doyle Bishop on my lunch hour. Alex bought me an emerald green silk dress that was the most beautiful dress I had ever seen, and a pair of matching green satin heels. I felt the most elegant woman in Seattle. And on that day, I think I was. The next night they were going to come for dinner at our apartment at 6:00. Though never fond of my mother, I had some strange subliminal need for her approval. For weeks before their arrival, I cleaned the apartment top to bottom, arranged all the towels mono-chromatically, raced home from work to cook the nicest dinner I knew how, set a pretty table, and on and on. At 6:00, no mother; 7:00, no mother. At 7:30 she phoned, saying they were busy partying with some friends, in Sheridan Beach. They wouldn't be able to make it to our apartment. I was crestfallen. They left town the next morning. I did not see them again for several years.

Roadblock

In the 60's, at the University of Washington, one had to success-fully complete three physical education courses for a degree. I passed swimming. No problem. I wanted to take tennis, but it never worked with my academic and work schedules. I signed up for Polka, thinking it dumb, but feasible. I flunked it. I had a hard time memorizing the patterns and I hated the music. I signed up for schottische, another no-brainer, but I flunked it. Same problem. So, I took Archery and passed it. Two down and one to go. Next, bowling. This would be easy. I was a decent bowler. My friends and I often went to the Magnolia Bowling Alley on McGraw Street. I averaged about 120. This should cinch my degree. Again, a glitch: our instructor insisted I was holding the ball wrong. Unless I held the ball the way she taught, she would not be able to pass me. I tried it her way. You had to get 70 points to pass with a D. I got 69. Flunked again.

Finally, I signed up for Golf in the Spring Quarter my Senior UW year, 1968. WHEW! I was the only one, in the class of 43 men, who got an A. Close call; I was running out of options!

My favorite area of study all through the University was art. Michael Spafford's course in Design thrilled me. I loved the History of Architecture and the History of Art. I also studied French, Italian, Spanish, 10 hours of Chaucer and a broad brush of Literature. I particularly loved Thomas Hardy and Faulkner. Thirty hours of Shakespeare from Angelo Pelligrini brought the old bard to life; Pelligrini teaching Shakespeare! Good combination. I purchased mostly used books; each volume became filled with marginal notes written during lectures. My so hard-fought-for B.A. was in Literature with a specialty in American Lit, Elementary and Secondary Education.

Graduation Day at the University of Washington in 1968, after nine long years of grinding away was truly festive. More than 5000 under graduates filled the venerable Hec Edmundson Pavillion, all tarted up in caps and gowns, our best shoes and stockings to walk across the stage. My sister Emmy drove up from Portland to cheer for me.

After the ceremony and speeches, the Literature graduates were invited over to the "Columns" behind Frosh Pond for a reception. I no sooner arrived than I noticed my ultimate savior, Dean Riley, walking toward me. "I knew you could make it, McQuesten. I'm very proud of your amazing progress, in spite of the fact you are working full time. You've done a remarkable job, despite those first 45 credits not boding well." I was tempted to hug him, but Dean Riley, being a proper sort, I thought better of it. I gave him a hardy hand shake. Frankly, I was glad it was over.

After graduation, Terry and I took a trip East with two other couples. Another classmate of ours, Norm Dicks, then an Aid to Senator Warren G. Magnuson, with Norms' wife, Suzie Callison, took us on tour of the Capitol Building, Rotunda, etc. When Norm turned around to show us something else, I turned back to Maggie's office, (which was exceedingly tidy) I pulled out the middle desk drawer for pencil and paper and wrote him a note: "Dear Maggie: Clean your desk – it's a mess! xoxo, dee" (It wasn't really….It was immaculate!)

When I reported my writing of this note to Norm, his eyes and mouth opened up with alarm: "dee, you can't do that! You will get me in terrible trouble with the BOSS"! He unlocked Maggie's door, dashed over and removed the note!

After sustaining too many black eyes, bruises and some hearing loss in my left ear and worse, at Terry's hand, I still cautiously de-cided not to leave him until I finished college. It would have been too confusing to try to muddle through a divorce and still be alert enough to study for exams, etc., working all the while three jobs *simultaneously.*

One night, shortly post-graduation, we were at dinner with some of his colleagues from Price Waterhouse. After dinner the men retired into the living room to discuss whatever men discussed and the women stayed in the dining room to discuss diaper rashes, formulas, breast feeding, etc. With no children, I was uninterested in much of the conversation, so I wandered into the living room where they were discussing politics and sat down on the fireplace hearth.

On the way home, Terry said: "You had no business coming into the living room where the men were talking. You should have stayed in the dining room with the women." I replied: "I want a divorce." He said:" WHAT!!!!! I said it again "I want a divorce. I am not happy. I want to raise a family, but I don't want to raise it with you." Terry had 5 reasons he didn't like children: They were messy, noisy, dirty, expensive, and would take too much of his time. I could have children if I wanted, but I was to keep them at my end of the house, as he was very busy in his den or on the golf course.

Not by design, I found myself pregnant after 5 years of marriage, but, 4 ½ months along, I began to hemorrhage and passed out. The next thing I knew was awakening in a dark, hospital room, in the middle of the night. There was a phone by my bed. I called Terry. He said "I would come to the hospital to see you, but I'm very busy at work. I will try to make it up to the hospital on my noon hour."

The Doctor who had performed surgery on me the night before, supposedly a D & C, was the head of Obstetrics, and Chief of Staff at Swedish Hospital. He was drunk. He had not noticed there was a second child. After excruciating labor pains two days later, I had a second child, a little boy, in my hospital bed all alone. The sight of that small baby, dead, devastated me beyond description.

The other person most upset, for all the wrong reasons, was my father-in-law, John, Chairman of the Board of Swedish Hospital. He implored me not to sue, as a lawsuit would be poor publicity for the hospital's fundraising campaign. I was too weak to sue, anyway. It wouldn't bring the twins back. I could barely do anything but cry.

My marriage was non-existent. Now the twins were gone; my life was a mess! On my last hospital day, Terry picked me up to drop me at home (during his lunch hour). On the way home, I told him I didn't want to live like this anymore. There was no companionship. There was no conversation. There was no friendship. At night after work he lived in his den with the door shut, instructing me not to bother him unless I had a very specific "agenda." He managed to come out of his den for the dinners I cooked, but at no other time.

For several months after the twins, I did not want to talk on the phone or answer the door. I had taken Incompletes in my University classes. What happened to those babies? Did they have souls? Were they in Heaven? Do they know who I am? Will I see them again? I was so overwhelmed I could barely function. Then, one day, I went to see my Pastor, Cannon Poland H. Miller at the Church of the Ascension Episcopal Church on Magnolia.

He gently explained to me, as I sat and wept at his desk, "One of the responsibilities of the Angels is to look after those babies who hadn't quite made it to earth; the Angels will nurture them, and take loving care of them until you get to Heaven."

Good theology or not, I felt better. I began to heal and take comfort that those children were not lost to me forever. I went back to school and finished my undergraduate degree.

The only vacation Terry and I ever took together was to the Bahamas in 1967. We stayed at a grand hotel in Nassau. I think it's now called the British Colonial. Terry had won some kind of contest at work, so his accounting firm paid for the trip. We played tennis on the hotel's red clay courts. That week Jackie Kennedy and Aristotle Onassis were in port on his enormous yacht. By coincidence Jackie and I were both wearing white cotton slacks, white long-sleeved cotton turtlenecks, white scarves and sun glasses. We were exactly the same size. The paparazzi followed me for three days, shooting pictures of me, thinking I was Jackie.

Otherwise our life together was consistent and disappointing. At 7:00 a.m. every Saturday morning, Terry's father picked him up for golf. He was gone all day while I did the house and yard chores and studied. On Sunday mornings at 7:00 his father picked him up for golf. He was gone again all day while I did the house and yard chores. . . and so it went, year after year.

Finally, one Mother's Day, after 8 years of this, his mother and father picked Terry up for golf at the Seattle Golf Club, leaving me home to cook Mother's Day dinner for seven: Terry's parents, his three siblings, Terry and I. His Mother, Margaret, said: "It's too bad you can't come, but you have a meal to cook." Though my salary Terry had used to pay the Golf Club Initiation and maintain the monthly dues, I was unwelcome. Also, at that time, I had learned quite a lot of golfing skill at UW. Dinner was already organized, the table set. I had the time to go, too, but I was unwelcome. Inconvenient.

That fateful day, I set a beautiful table with flowers from my yard, prepared a nice meal and wrapped a present for Margaret. I had intended to serve dinner when they all arrived home. By the time I was finished frosting the cake, I decided I was finished. On second thought, before I left the house, at the last minute, I picked up

Margaret's beautifully wrapped Mother's Day gift from the dining room table, and kept it for myself. It was a gorgeous green basket of strawberry-shaped pink guest soaps in a nest. I left before they returned from the Golf Club to search for an apartment. I did not return until after 9:00 when everyone was gone; I did, however, do all the clean-up, wash and iron the linens and put everything away.

For 10 years, beginning when Terry and I were first dating, I had been considerate and thoughtful of his parents. For ten years, whenever I had stopped by their home, John greeted me with "Hi Stupid!" The only stupid thing about me was putting up with Terry's and his father's negatively demeaning behavior. When Terry and I were married, they asked me to promise to put him through School his last three years of undergraduate school. I promised. And I did. I financed Terry's last three years of college for his B.A. in Mathematics at the University of Washington. I kept my promise at great personal sacrifice. His dad might have said "Thank you for seeing to it that my son achieved his college degree." He might have said "Thank you for taking on the home and yard chores so Gary and I could play golf all weekend every weekend." There were a lot of things he could have said, had he any grace at all, instead of "Hi, Stupid!"

My attorney advised me that I was entitled to 50% of Terry's Retirement pay because I put him through 3 years of college. I refused my attorney's urging because I was terror-stricken at the thought of what he might do if I agreed to that. I declined. I did what I had to do to escape and be safe.

Remembering now the painful time of that first marriage I am amazed at how I duplicated in the relationship with Terry and his family, the life I had lived with my birth mother – being called names, unimaginable physical and emotional abuse, succumbing to total financial dependence; i.e., allowing Terry to have all my pay-checks while he, in turn, "*allowed*" me 25 cents a day for food, letting slowly slip away most every sense of self-worth, even as I succeeded quite well in other dimensions of my life at work or in society, holding responsible jobs, finishing school, making friends.... but never able to acknowledge the gifts I had, the gift I was.

I had been, perhaps, an inconvenient wife, but no more!

dee McQuesten; University of Washington Graduation...1968

Stairway in U.W. Suzzallo Library leading up to Study Stacks

CHAPTER SIX

Post Graduation;
Post Marriage

A short time after Graduation I got a call from Kelly Girls' temporary service, asking if I could work the following morning at Seattle Mental Health on Capitol Hill. They needed someone for just one day to answer the phone and do the initial Intake documents for walk-in patients. Unknown to me, their long-time receptionist, had been attacked that day by a patient. She ran out the front door screaming and never came back.

The mother of one of my high school classmates, Gary Tuininga, was responsible for staffing at Seattle Mental Health. Within a week or two, Mrs. Tuininga called me, with reports that I had been very good with clients: Would I stay permanently? I had absolutely no training for what was, essentially, social work, with the most challenging responsibility of handling the incoming suicide lines for our entire catchment area, which included a very depressed downtown Seattle, Capitol Hill, Magnolia and Queen Anne. This was my first exposure to prostitutes and pimps; never before had I interacted with tall leather-bound pimps in platform shoes, shades and hats. A variety of other patients walked through our doors physically injured from domestic violence, or in need of counseling for drugs, depression, suicide attempts or a myriad of other too human conditions.

I had a lot to learn about many human sufferings I knew nothing about. I am grateful for that experience.

I did not rush into the job, but, upon reflection, decided it would be a challenge and it was. I learned much about myself, life, and loss, but after, two years, I needed a change of scenery from a very pressing and depressing job. Frequently I spent over an hour, sometimes two, on the line with one suicide call.

When I was working "Intake" at Seattle Mental Health, I often would lunch at the main hospital with the other staff and the patients. The meals were excellent and affordable. One afternoon, shortly after I finished my meal, I was standing at the south windows overlooking Madison Street (across from what is now Trader Joe's) above the No. 11 Bus Stop.

Notorious Pansy and son George, two perennial characters on Capitol Hill through the 60's-80, were waiting at the stop. George, in his always rumpled white slacks and pink sport coat with a fake daisy in the breast pocket, looked up at me and began pointing his finger, asking his mother to look at the "Inmate!" Being pointed to an laughed at by George for acting crazy was a new low . . .or high?

I lived just one block from the Institute on 17th Avenue in a 2-story townhouse. One evening after dinner, while Janie Carlson Williams, a house guest, was taking a bath upstairs, an unfamiliar man appeared at my open front door. He said, "Is that Jensen's car out your back window?" I turned to look backward through my dining room window to see my own car parked at the curb. As I did so, his large hand grabbed my throat from behind and began choking me. Very strong in those days, I fought like a wild animal, knocking pictures off the walls, furniture over on the floor, etc. But, eventually,

I was unconscious. When I awoke, perpetrator standing over me, Janie was running down the stairway in her robe. I bolted out the kitchen door to the house across the street, where a neighbor called 911.

The assailant escaped out my living room door, driving quickly away. SPD told me, during an interview the following morning, the person who attacked me had gone on to rape two different women on Queen Anne the same night. They also urged me to move immediately, since I could identify a very dangerous man.

In 1969, I moved from Capitol Hill into the Lake Court Apartments on 43rd Avenue East in Madison Park, a neighborhood where I have remained the rest of my life, except for 9 months in Cambridge. Lake Court itself became a bit unnerving because the resident manager, Mr. Schwartz, was a thief. He entered apartments during the day while residents were at work and helped himself to whatever seemed valuable to him. One day, when I was home sick from work, he walked right into my bedroom. He was surprised to see me. It was the 15th of the month, so when I asked what he was doing. He replied that he came to collect the rent. I reminded him it wasn't due until the first and asked him to leave. Over a period of time, my grandfather's Paganini violin with his lovely hand-made-by-himself as a child, case; my great-grand grandfather's monogram engraved gold pocket watch and my red leather loafers; all disappeared, presumably into his light-fingers. I had no way to prove it his thievery, but several neighbors had the same experience.

Harvard, Baby, Here I Come!

Though I earned very little at Seattle Mental Health doing Intake and Suicide Lines, I had saved enough for a one-way ticket to Boston with $43 left over. My friend, Candy Todd, who graduated from

Wellesley, planned to return to New England. She encouraged me to join her. Single, unattached, free, I did just that in 1970.

I lived across the Lake Court walk from Gretchen Mathers who had a friend looking for an apartment in the Park. She rented mine. I had spoken to my Supervisor at Seattle Mental Health, who said he thought it sounded like a wonderful experience. He cheered for me! With only 48 hours to plan my move, I loaned my car to a friend, packed one large suitcase and off I went, scrambling to get the last flight to Boston on a Friday afternoon. Racing up to the ticket counter, I asked for a one-way ticket. The agent said: "One way, are you *sure?*" I was. I ran all the way through the airport to the loading ramp. Last one aboard before take-off. Whew. Barely made it.

A bit of irony: before I left, I asked a close friend from college make some calls for me and cancel a few appointments. The last name on the list was Terry, telling him I had moved to Boston. Terry said: "My appointment with dee McQuesten was cancelled some time ago. Would you like to go to dinner?" A few days later they were married barefoot on the beach in Mexico! That marriage, too, ended in divorce.

Though this connection between Terry and my college friend was quite accidental on my part, I do delight in connecting people. I have introduced 26 couples who have eventually married; 25 of whom are still married today.

Careful with my last $43, I took a train from the Boston's Logan Airport into town from which I called a friend attending Tufts University, Boo Edmunds. I stayed with her for a few days while looking for a job. Before leaving Seattle, I had read that Boston was desperate for substitute teachers – my intended job. At the University of Washington, I had completed both the elementary and secondary education curricula, as Grandpa had urged me over and over: "Get a teaching degree because you never know when you might have to support a family." I had not yet done the fifth year that Washington State required, but was assured in a phone call the Boston Public School Department, they did not have that requirement for substitute teachers.

Filled with hope and confidence, I marched into the Boston Public School Office on Monday morning. OOPS! I had forgotten to pack everything needed -- my Diploma and transcripts. Never mind. While I waited for the University of Washington to communicate with the Boston School District, I sought some "temp" work. Advertisements in The Boston Globe and subways for The Skill Bureau claimed they hired the smartest and most talented temps. Thinking they might have interesting temp jobs, I found their office and took the typing and shorthand exams. Before I even left the premises, the president of the Skill Bureau, Sander Poritzky, came out of his back office saying he would like to talk with me. He told me he had just completed the renovation of a second branch of the Skill Bureau in Cambridge on Brattle Street, near the famous Harvard Kiosk. He was searching for a Vice President to run this Harvard Square operation on Brattle Street near the Coop. Having quickly perused my resume, he thought I might be a good fit. He said he would call my former, long-time employer, Eddie Carlson, President at Westin Hotels and United Airlines simultaneously, the following day for a reference. After he and Mr. Carlson spoke the following day, Sander offered me the job.

One of my responsibilities was interviewing applicants applying for various temporary clerical/office positions. One afternoon a tall, slender well-dressed woman arrived; stunning beauty, with long dark hair and a French accent. Francoise filled out the application and left. The next afternoon she phoned, inviting me for drinks and dinner that evening with her and her boyfriend at an upscale Cambridge restaurant.

When I arrived, at 5:30, they were both sipping water. I ordered a glass of red wine remarking that I, the only one imbibing, felt like a lush. Francoise replied they never drank alcohol before sex. I asked if we were still planning on dinner. The boyfriend explained that they also didn't eat dinner until after sex, as food and alcohol dull sexual pleasures. I was somewhat confused by their personal sharing . . . too much information! They explained they would like me to join them at Francoise's apartment for a *menage a trois!*

A simple Yakima/Rimrock/Seattle girl, I naively, thought maybe that was some kind of eastern or French dinner.

Finally, I realized their true plan for the evening. I explained I was somewhat old-fashioned and would not be any fun for them; besides, I had a Lit class on Thomas Hardy at 7:30, so they would have to excuse me. Undaunted, Francoise called me two more times. Did I misspell "NO?"

My work in Harvard Square was super, but with no friends, nothing to do in the evenings, and since I was in the neighborhood, I decided to try a class or two at Harvard. Women were not allowed on the Harvard (pronounced Havud) campus in the day time; I could only go at night, anyway. Our classes were on Mass Ave in office buildings. With my undergrad degree already in hand, I took more literature classes for both enrichment and enjoyment....and to perhaps meet some new people. The Harvard experience was, in many ways, a tremendous experience for this Yakima girl who had rarely left her familiar Northwest.

For example, one day, because I typed faster than most, and did so accurately, at about 200 wpm, I got a surprise call telling me the man who had for years been typing the play-by-plays for the Harvard Football Team was in the hospital; they needed someone to fill in for the season. Thus began my season working for the Harvard Athletic Department, in the top of the Harvard Stadium for every Saturday home game, the first woman in history allowed in the Harvard Press Box. The A.P and U.P.I. men tried desperately to clean up their language. I insisted their language did not bother me; I was only there for a few short weeks. The words went right over my naive head, as I didn't understand the slang, anyway.

One of the perks of living on Beacon Hill in Boston, when I first arrived, had been that each week Arthur Fiedler performed behind my Charles Street Flat in the Boston Symphony Shell on the Charles River bank. We'd take a blanket and a bottle of water and watch the whole performance. There were never any charges. A great thrill!!!!

On Charles Street in Boston, I lived only a block from Ted and Joan Kennedy. I frequently ran into Joan at the local bodega. Then one afternoon, as I emerged from the Subway in Cambridge, on my way home from work, a well-dressed woman approached me, asking if I would volunteer on Teddy's Senatorial race. I was assigned to Joan Kennedy's upcoming Sunday afternoon tea event. My assignment was to stick close to her, introducing her to the afternoon tea attendants, by name. The Sunday I was to help Joan, I was sick and missed the event. But I spent several interesting months volunteering in other ways for the campaign. A talent for remembering names and faces has been valuable on several levels to the 21 campaigns for which I have volunteered.

After just a couple of months commuting between Cambridge and Beacon Hill, I moved into a fascinating a co-op with 11 others, a mixture of students and graduates at 88 Chilton Street, Cambridge.

There I was privileged to interact with brilliant, talented Harvard, Wellesley and Tufts students, one of whom became a lifelong friend. We played tennis together, ate banana splits at the local Farrell's Ice Cream Parlor, where I learned about chocolate "Jimmies." We attended student parties. My favorite housemate, Jane Williams, eventually married Fritz Reed, a star on the Harvard football team alongside his roommate, Tommy Lee Jones. They both played in the now famous Harvard-Yale game, which they "won" 29 to 29. A movie was made of that game and that unusual team. Fritz ran a fumble back for a touchdown in the final minutes, of that unforgotten contest. Fritz went on to Harvard Law School, became CFO of Wendy's, dying very young of a heart attack.

I worked in the neighborhood, Harvard Square, as they partially filmed the movie, "Love Story" starring Ryan O'Neal and Ali McGraw. One noon hour I noticed the crew filming me, following on for two blocks as I walked out to lunch. Sadly, whatever they had in mind ended on the cutting room floor before the film was released.

I sat near Ali MacGraw several years later in the 6th row in a New York theater, when I went to see Dustin Hoffman do "Death of a Salesman." She hadn't aged a bit, was as beautiful as ever, and, surprisingly, failed to recognize me from the film we almost shared!

A friend from my office building, Glen Howard, a gifted vocalist from Birmingham, Alabama, was, while still in school, a warm-up act for some great performers – the renowned "Sha-Na-Na's" and Ike and Tina Turner – at their Harvard Stadium concerts. The evening of Glen's show with Sha-Na-Na and the Turners, late, as I was closing up the Harvard Square office of The Skill Bureau, four young men charged up the stairs and dispersed widely throughout my large office; one of them flashing a knife at me and two of them rifling through my purse. They took my wallet and my keys. Most hurtful was that in my wallet was my opening night ticket, for the Sha Na Na's and Turners at the Harvard Stadium.

Glen was also the conductor of the Harvard singing club and a Cantor in a Temple in Birmingham. He spoke five languages and directed Harvard's Hasty Pudding musical group, "The Krokodiloes." Simultaneously, in 1970 he was directing Radcliffe's production of " Funny Girl," maintaining a 4.0 grade average and working part time. I kept in touch with Glen for many years as he went on to clerk for Judge Edenfield in the 5th Circuit, then became the youngest partner in a Washington, D.C., firm.

Multi-tasking still, he guest conducted and sang with the Robert Shaw Chorale in the Kennedy Center and, on Sundays, produced a radio show for Mobile Oil, entitled "Classics Illustrated," featuring Brazilian music one Sunday, German the next, and so on. His wife, Lauren Feinstein, another highly-educated and equally talented person, was the International Trade partner in a separate Washington, D.C. law firm, while taking jazz dancing at night and co-parenting their son.

Back to Seattle

Though I loved the Harvard/Cambridge/Boston days, I did get terribly homesick and worried that if something happened to Gran, I would not be there, so I moved home after three quarters. Back in Seattle, after my sojourn in the wider word, I sadly discovered there was not a New York Times to be found ANYWHERE! When I desperately needed a hit, I drove out to the Sea-Tac Airport, waited for the non-stop red eye to arrive from JFK Airport in Manhattan. The stewards let me board the planes after they were emptied to discover a New York Times....a little trick I learned from Paul Barrett.

The 70's became for me a widely mixed bag of different jobs, trying to figure out what I liked best, in addition to picture framing, which had become my hobby. I took classes at Cornish College of the Arts and buried myself in creativity.

My most interesting job was as Case Manager for the Economic Development Council. I became convinced of and concerned that the Flying Service operating out of Juanita, flying to the San Juan Islands, should be shifted to somewhere on Lake Union – much more convenient for their passengers. I went to the restaurant next to Franco's Hidden Harbor, at the south end of the lake, called a meeting of both parties and made all the arrangements. Easily done, as the restaurant had a handy dock that could be used for take-offs and landings.

I had a couple other jobs, including Secretary for the Epiphany School in Madrona, working for Mr. Spock, Headmaster and brother to the celebrated child authority, Doctor Spock. He was growly and generally unpleasant. One afternoon Peggy Dion, one of the teachers, came to my office and invited me over for cake in the school building behind my office to celebrate someone's birthday. I went for about 10 minutes. When I returned, Mr. Spock was in a rage. "Didn't I tell you never to leave your desk except to use the Ladies' Room? YOU'RE FIRED!!!" I loved the children, but Mr. Spock was so acidic I was actually relieved. I had only been there three months.

A New Little Family and Saving the Market

In the early 70's, Seattle faced a civic crisis. I, alongside 144 volunteers under the driven determination of architect Victor Steinbrueck, door-belled all of King County hoping to maintain the venerable Pike Place Market as a market and not have it torn down by developers. The "Save-The-Market" supporters were victorious, saving what was then and has become even more so since, our city's premier tourist attraction and public treasure. After the campaign, I was invited to work in the Market.

In that role of working for the Market Renovation Director, George Rolfe, I learned a lot of the Market history. A man came in one day wanting to open a space to sell coffee – only coffee. No one thought he could make a go of just selling coffee. He did well, expanded his business, and shortly thereafter turned over the management of his now 3 shops, named "Starbucks," to a New York up and comer, Howard Schultz!

One day a co-worker in the Market compound, Michelle Clise, came to my office announcing that, since I lived alone, I needed a dog. She had found one, dirty and skinny and frightened, stuck out on a traffic island on Aurora Avenue. She insisted I come to her home after work and meet this little dog, an Australian Sheltie. It was love at first bark! In my townhouse on Newton Street in Madison Park pets were not allowed. Pleading, I called my landlord, Hugh Ainslie. He met Alice, a completely house broken, 3 or 4 year-old, and agreed she could stay. I hadn't had a dog since I was a toddler, so neglected to notice obvious parameters like the garbage can in the kitchen. When I arrived home from work the first night Alice lived with me, I discovered she had pulled apart my garbage and spread tomato sauce all over the brand new carpet that the landlord had installed the week before. Though sure I'd be evicted, Hugh was unbelievably nice about it.

Only days later, Carolyn Temple, another co-worker at the Market, shared that a cousin's cat had just had kittens two weeks prior. She insisted Alice should not be alone all day and that dogs and cats get along well when they live together. We went out north of the

University Village to meet one of the little creatures; I brought him home, sick as he was with ear mites. I had to administer a prescription in his ears every three hours for three weeks. I named him Mazel tov, believing him lucky to get me for a mom who would take good care of him. He was Jewish and my dog, Alice, was Catholic. I thought it important to have an ecumenical home. When I brought Mazel tov home, he climbed right into Alice's basket, snuggled up to her immediately adopting her as his mother. Alice stared at the ceiling, pretending it wasn't happening.

From that first moment on, Mazel tov mimicked Alice, doing everything she did. When we went for walks, Maz always went with us. When Alice and I walked to the Madison Park Bakery mornings to get a cup of coffee. Maz always came along. The Bakery had a Dutch door with a windowsill on each side of the door. Alice jumped up on one sill; Maz on the other. The early morning bakery patrons always patted each one on the head and greeted them as they entered the door. Before I caught the bus to work, I walked Alice home. Maz set out to cruise the neighborhood.

New Church

From my grandmother's prayers on her knees at my bed side to the frequent search for a church home to escape to from my birthmother, a religious home and community of faith has been an enduring, and even life-giving dimension of my life.

While living in Madison Park I had transferred my membership from the Magnolia Church of the Ascension Episcopal Church to the Church of Epiphany Episcopalian Church in Madrona. Each Sunday, only 3 or 4 other people were at the 10:00 or 11:00 services – a different three or four each week. Church had become a lonely experience. When I lamented about this Gran kept urging, yet again in my life: "Diane, Dear, you need to find a church home. You are alone in a big city with no family. You need a church community." I looked around. I visited the Quaker Friends Church, Temple de Hirsch, University Presbyterian, Methodist, Congregational, Lutheran, etc. Nothing fit.

Then, one Palm Sunday, I asked my next door neighbors, Mary Kay Dyckman and Libby Moscardini, if I could ride with them to St. Patrick's on Capitol Hill near Roanoake Park. The Church was packed! We barely found a place to sit. As the music began, a very short angelic-looking priest processed down the center aisle in white robes, wearing a million dollar smile, with a halo-like circle of white hair that matched his robes. Father Joe Kramis.

The service was lively. The music was spirited and energetic. Father Joe gave a homily I remember to this day about the Transfiguration. After Mass, I asked Libby and Mary Kay to introduce me as we went down the front steps. I stopped to talk with Father Joe and told him I was searching for a new church home and asked to visit with him?

He said that a week from Thursday would be good, after the Easter celebrations were over. Come for supper at the Rectory. Really? I didn't know women could go into a Rectory. Nancy McQuiggan, head housekeeper and cook, made us a lovely dinner. After supper, Fr. Joe said "Let's go out in the back yard and visit." Joe didn't have a lot of excess money to maintain the garden and lawn; the grass was almost two feet high. He set up two aluminum lawn chairs, with turquoise and white woven plastic seats and backs, totally tattered and half shredded. We sat down amidst the tall grass, almost knee to knee. "Now then, "Joe said, "Tell me what you are looking for in a church home."

That was easy. I had a list of 8 requirements: A church that wasn't judgmental and didn't claim "Catholicism and Christianity are the only way;" that believed other faiths were viable, that we are all God's children, that all humans are equal - had an active community where people got together and supported each other, and where everyone is welcoming and welcomed. "dee McQuesten," Joe said, "You have come to the right place!"

Joe taught a class in the rectory, beginning in two weeks each Tuesday night, on what it meant to be a Catholic. Would I like to join his class? Yes, I thought that would be nice. I did. I attended for a whole year. At the end of the year, Joe said, "What do you think, dee? Are you ready to join the church?" I replied that I liked it a lot, but wanted to be absolutely sure. I did not want to ever have to change churches again. Could I take his class one more year? "Fine," he said, "You are welcome to do that. We'll see you Tuesday night."

Another year of Tuesdays and Thursdays. At the end of the second year, same question: "Well, dee, what do you think?" Same answer. "You know, Joe, I just need to be absolutely sure. This is an important commitment for me. Do you mind if I take your class just one more year?"

And so it went, every Tuesday and Thursday from 7:00 to 9:00 for a third year. At the end, the repeat question from Joe: "Well, dee?" "Yes", I said. This feels like home to me." "Terrific," said Joe, giving me an exuberant 'high-five,' "Now you are a Kramis Catholic!"

At the Easter Vigil in 1978, I became a Catholic. A good decision never to be regretted, but celebrated over and over. One of the best decisions of my life.

*Placque at Harvard Gate, established in
1636....Cambridge, Massachusets*

CHAPTER SEVEN

The Single Life

During my single years, I tried a lot of varied jobs and industries. I joined Honey Hansen Travel Agency as a travel agent trainee, was an anti-trust litigation paralegal for Helsell, Fetterman, Martin, Todd and Hokanson, then did sales for Phil Smart Mercedes, hoping to save enough money for law school at Hastings in San Francisco.

One of my 70's adventures was to buy part of a sailboat, a 27 footer. I loved heavy weather sailing. I learned sailing as a member of the Corinthian Yacht Club and by crewing races on other people's sailboats. I took the Coast Guard class on Navigation. My boat's name was "Buckwheat;" I always took my dog, Alice, who had tremendous sea legs and never once fell overboard.

London and Paris – Tea at "The Browns"

In 1972, free to travel, I ventured off to Europe, very anxious to spend a month in London. By happenstance, my seat mate was the Seattle Symphony's Concertmaster (first Violinist Vilem Sokol) on the flight to London. I asked him where to stay. He suggested a bureau office where I could register for a room with a family. I did so and reserved a room with the Mom and Pop Jones household in Clapham Common. They were wonderful and accommodating, giving me, among many other new experiences, my first sample of fried bread. EEEEUUUWWWW!

One leisurely afternoon I treated myself to Tea at the Browns boutique Hotel. Tea was a lovely, almost fairy tale-like experience.

"The Browns plays the role of hotel so unobtrusively that one could almost accidentally feel they were in someone's private home", it states on their brochure. I could not resist.

"This hotel was opened in 1837 by John Brown, a gentleman's gentleman, whose wife, Sarah, had been Lady's Maid to Lady Byron, widow of the poet. They acquired four Exquisite Georgian residences on Dover Street and divided them into 16 suites, each with a servant's room and a courier's room. A further seven Georgian homes on Albemarle Street, directly behind Dover (off Piccadilly) were later used to expand the hotel. Guests rented a suite and ate in their own private dining room.

Regular American visitors were the Vanderbilts, Rockefellers and Cabots. Theodore Roosevelt was married there. Several years later on, Mr. and Mrs. Franklin Roosevelt honeymooned at The Browns. Generally speaking, The Browns is the haunt of English country families.

Tea is served from 4 – 6 in a large drawing room with tawny wood paneling, gentle lighting and easy chairs covered in William Morris Chintz. It is a restful tea; so restful, in fact, that Agatha Christie wrote one of her novels, "Murder on the Orient Express", I believe, while sitting there. "Tea?", asked the waiter discreetly. This important point established, he melted away as though ashamed of having disturbed my peace. When it appeared – cucumber, egg, ham and sardine sandwiches, brown bread and butter, jam and cakes, a reassuringly traditional tea, it was laid down with a flourish. The final touch was a embroidered starched beige and cream linen napkin, matching the tablecloth, which he plopped ceremoniously onto my Royal Worcester plate!" Next, off to the Royal Ballet.

One afternoon a few days later, I rather randomly looked over some notices on a Kiosk. I saw the Grand Opera in Paris was performing Rigoletto, my favorite opera. The next morning, on a spur of the proper moment, I hopped a train ride up to the Cliffs of Dover, bought a ticket on the Hovercraft to Calais, and found myself in Paris – again without accommodations.

On the Hovercraft, I met three people from Australia, all needing a place to stay. Someone recommended a small boutique hotel; we, so caught a cabbie and off we went! Curiously enough, for 3 days in Paris, I did not encounter one soul who spoke English. Fortunately, I had had two years of French, way back when, but it got me through.

In the morning, I caught another cab to the Grand Opera to buy a ticket for "Rigoletto." Alas, there had been a severe rainstorm and a portion of the roof had caved in just this week; the opera would not re-open for at least two more weeks.

Extremely disappointed, but still excited to be in Paris for the first time, I wandered around the theater areas and discovered that, as it was Saturday, there were no tickets to be had for any evening performances but, of all things, "Bonjour *Dolleeee*" in French, which I attended and thoroughly enjoyed, despite my bumbling French. Prior to the 8:00 performance, I treated myself to supper at an upscale French Café.

When it was time to return to my hotel, I caught a cabbie and said to him, "Please take me to...?" I had failed to write down the name of the hotel or the address. The befuddled but extremely kind cabbie toured Paris for an hour and 45 minutes until finally guessing which hotel I had departed from, boasting only 6 rooms, – a near miracle – and a miraculously *large* cab fare!

The next day, the cab driver taking me to the Orly airport asked, if I had done everything in Paris I hoped for. I told him of my disappointment at not seeing "Rigoletto". He replied that he sang the baritone part in "Rigoletto". "Would I like to hear it?"

For forty-five minutes, I heard firsthand the most beautiful voice I had ever heard treating me to my own private opera! This great singer drove a cab to support his family, hoping to save enough to join the San Francisco Opera one day; I hope he did. I wish I had asked his name!

During my single years, before and after my marriage to Terry, I had an eventful, sometimes humorous, sometimes frightening, always interesting dating life. In my late twenties and thirties I was still searching for who I was or ought to be and with whom. The uncertainty began even earlier.

My first serious dating exploration goes back to high school, when a friend, Jerry Landeen, arranged a blind date for me with a friend of his – John Ruud, a Lincoln High School student a year ahead of me. John was terrific! I admired him enormously. One of the occasions I recall clearly was the night he was a groomsman for Earl Palmer, Pastor of the University Presbyterian Church. We attended a lot of Young Life Meetings together and took three trips to Camp Malibu in Canada; one as a guest and two as a worker. John was one of the good guys and I was completely smitten. One summer afternoon, just before my senior year, Paul Barrett and his best friend, Jerry Lundquist, came to visit at my home on Magnolia. Jerry brought me a gigantic stuffed rabbit almost as tall as I was. We were out in my back yard. They had been there about 10 minutes when John Ruud came by. Misunderstanding the situation, John thought Jerry Lundquist (whom I didn't really even know; had only seen one time with Paul) was a hidden boyfriend.

In that era, 1957. we were clearly indoctrinated that "a young lady never telephones a young man." I wanted sooooo badly to call John and explain the awkward situation, but I feared doing so was inappropriate; that he would think me forward. I was sadly short of self confidence in those days or I would have called him. We never spoke again, as John completely disappeared –I didn't ever hear from him. My first experience of a broken heart.

When I got to the U.W, Jerry again arranged a blind date for me with Jack Nilles, his Fiji fraternity brother. Jack, just returned from the Military, was beginning college. I found him interesting, but he never called again; apparently I was not as interesting.

While I was working Crisis Intake at Seattle Mental Health, Janie Carlson, daughter of my long-time boss, Eddie Carlson, and her mother, Nel, arranged a blind date for me with Janie's brother. He picked me up at my Lake Court Apartment. We walked over to the Attic Tavern for a burger. About half-way through mine, my date said, "How do you spend your evenings?" I reported that I played a lot of tennis and sometimes attended Young Republican Meetings. He was HORRIFIED! "How can you possibly waste your time on an organization like that?" He rushed me back to my apartment, abruptly ending the evening. Polarization even 40 years ago!

Years later, when I was living in Cambridge, however, he and his then wife, Maggie Carlson (Maggie – now an MSNBC political reporter) invited me to come to Washington, D.C. for Thanksgiving weekend, which I did, along with Ann and Eben Carlson and some other Seattle people.

Also, while in Cambridge, the owner of our Co-op house, Bob, arranged a blind date for me with the Publisher of the Boston alternative newspaper, "Boston After Dark," an entertainment paper of theatre reviews, museum events, etc. He was an extremely intelligent and worldly fellow, whom I liked a lot. But three weeks later, the same week the publisher moved into our co-op on Chilton Street, I went home for Christmas and never returned. I think my move was partially in fear that if I stayed I would become romantically involved and might never return to the Northwest and, especially, never again be near my precious Gran.

In 1969, I accepted a blind date with Ben Johnson. Off to the Attic again for another hamburger. Ben asked in-depth questions about my church affiliation. At that time I was a member of the Epiphany Church and occasionally attended St. Mark's. Ben was disappointed that I was weak in the church department, being scarcely a part-time attendee. He let me know that my part-time church habits were unacceptable. Bombed again! Only a 30-minute hamburger once more.

Another time, in 1969, some long term friends had someone they wanted me to meet, Merlin Hickle. Merlin picked me up one Saturday night and took me to what was thought by others, and certainly seemed to me, a pornographic movie, "I Am Curious Yellow." Then he took me to the Royal Fork, an all-you-can-eat restaurant on 45th Street in Seattle near the theatre. (I have a somewhat disgusted memory of Merlin returning to the buffet six times for more creamed corn!) On Monday, while I was at my desk on Christmas Eve at Seattle Mental Health, my phone rang. It was Merlin, asking: "What kind of flowers do you like?" I like daisies," I replied. "Do you like orchids?" he inquired. "No, I really don't." Just then, the front door opened. A delivery man handed me a gigantic bouquet of purple and white orchids! Merlin never called again. I was mortified beyond belief, incapable of any appropriate apology!

My saddest dating experience came in the 70's, when I was managing Slade Gorton's Campaign Office. Ruthie Yoniyama, an assistant to Dan Evans' gubernatorial Office in Olympia, and I became good friends. Slade and Dan, now political allies, had been college roommates. The two campaigns, running simultaneously, worked closely together.

Ruthie asked if I would accompany a member of Dan's Olympia staff, a man named Ben, to a reception for Happy and Governor Rockefeller. Ben was a dream date, a terrific conversationalist; another super-bright companion. We enjoyed the same music and composers. He invited me to dinner a few of weeks later. He was planning to drive up from Olympia and pick me up on Saturday night.

I forgot!

My sister, Em, showed up by surprise on that same Saturday morning, saying let's drive down to the ocean and spend the night. She was in the early stages of MS, but could still drive. Em and I were very close. I was sooo happy to see her, I totally forgot that I had a date that night.

As we drove through Olympia, towards the ocean, I remembered. OOPS! I had agreed to have dinner with Ben. We drove rapidly to a gas station to check the phone book. No luck. I called 'Information,' no luck. I looked in my wallet in case I had Ben's card. No luck.

On to the ocean, me with a heavy heart, torn between thinking I would not see that much more of Em, not knowing what MS meant either short or long term.... oh dear, I really did like Ben.

When we arrived back at my apartment on Sunday afternoon, there was a new long-play record album at my door by "Ravel", that we had spoken of with mutual fondness, and a bouquet of now very dead flowers. I felt terrible. I tried right away to call him from home, but he did not answer and would not call me back. I never got a chance to explain, or apologize, there really being no excuse, except my scattered brain!

Salt to these wounds, six months later Ben did call. He wanted me to go on a blind date with his best friend, a psychiatrist in Tacoma. I agreed with a heavy heart. I tried to explain what happened, but he was not interested in what I had to say. It did not go well with his friend either when he arrived one Saturday night. The doorbell rang. I answered the door in a dress and heels. I looked down. There was my date, several inches shorter than I and a brand new silver Porsche at the curb.

He asked if I cared where we dined; I said I was happy anywhere. This quite professional if very short psychiatrist said he had a favorite place; off we went to Ivar's Acres of Clams, the original Restaurant under the Viaduct on the Seattle waterfront. My date ordered a huge platter of fried clam strips which arrived instantly, smelling like they had been cooked the previous decade. He stopped talking. He began immediately devouring the entire platter, while licking the fingers of both hands vigorously with every bite. My dinner hadn't arrived. After watching him for a few minutes, I hovered between chagrined and appalled. Quickly I said: "Please don't take this personally, but I have a severe headache... No, don't get up! There is a cab stand at the curb. I'll catch it and call you next week." I ran (literally) out of the restaurant and was home exactly 23 minutes after he had picked me up! Shortest, if not the worst date ever.

Several years later I was freelancing as a Litigation Paralegal at the Perkins Law Firm. Ben had an office there. I passed him in the hallway. I said hello; he pretended he didn't recognize me. He did not respond. I am clearly on his "do not call" list.

While Ruthie Yoniyama was managing Dan Evans' Campaign Office on Lenora Street and I was managing Slade Gorton's office in the Seattle Tower Building, we often ran back and forth with envelopes, address lists, etc. She had another idea for my dating life. She had asked me to consider a date with a good looking law school student who was an Evans Campaign Volunteer. She pointed him out. He was indeed a nice appearing fellow in sport coat and tie, socializing with the other volunteers. However, just then I was dating Slade's campaign manager, so was luckily unavailable. The good looking volunteer in a sport coat and tie was, I discovered later, Ted Bundy!

Obviously, not all my experiences when single were good.

Life-Threatening Moments

One morning, in the wee hours, my dog Alice was barking loudly downstairs in the kitchen. Clearly, someone was trying to get into our townhouse on Newton Street through the kitchen window. Mazel tov had his own entrance through that window, which could have been easily removed, allowing access for an adult. I raced over and locked my bedroom door and put up the ironing board in front of my raised window. I was afraid to open my bedroom door and let Alice in, as someone could be coming up the stairs by this point. Alice was on her OWN!!!!

I crawled up on the ironing board and out onto the roof in nothing but my yellow nightgown. I stuck to the frozen icy roof. Mary Kay Dyckman, next door, heard the ruckus and called 911. Very soon, two very tall cops built like NFL lineman arrived at my front door. They checked the back door, encountering my other neighbor, Charlie, approaching my back patio in his white jockey shorts and tee shirt brandishing a butcher knife. There were large footprints in the snow below my kitchen window.

One of the cops leaned back against the kitchen stove and began to imitate "Garfield" from the newspaper cartoon to help me stop shaking. Within 2 days, the story of the break in and the policeman who calmed me down by imitating Garfield, was in the Seattle P.I. I was at Frederick & Nelson a couple of days later. When I was paying for an item, the clerk said to me, "Oh, you're dee McQuesten. I read about you in yesterday's P.I. paper! Scary stuff!"

One November windy rainy night as I exited the King County Courthouse on 3rd and Cherry after my law class, carrying a number of heavy law books, notebooks, purse, etc., to wait for the No. 11 bus, an elderly woman pushing a grocery cart approached me. She said, "Can I have a cigarette?" "Sorry, I don't smoke," I replied. She hauled off with her right fist and knocked me clear into the rushing muddy gutter, law books and papers all over the street; me on my hands and knees in the dirt and filth! As she clubbed me with her right fist, she uttered, "Don't you lecture me on morality!" Then, she was gone, along with her grocery cart of valuables, in a heartbeat, disappearing into the dark night.

The very next afternoon I was delivering documents to a major law firm downtown. This same woman, grocery cart and all, was sitting in their reception area. I inquired of the receptionist who she might be, mentioning my encounter the previous night. The receptionist said she was the mother of one of their partners. He and his affluent brother had tried for years to buy her a nice home and move her inside, but she liked it outside!

While I was working at the Pike Market in 1974, the Head Security Guard came to my desk one afternoon, announcing he would be walking me to my car, saying he was somewhat psychic and felt I was in danger. So, off we went at 5:00 to the Market Garage without incident. That night, however, was a different story.

At 10:00 on a beautiful October night, I walked my dog Alice before bedtime. At the alley on East Blaine Street, between 43rd and 42nd, two men jumped out. One held a gun to my forehead. The other poked my white raincoat in the stomach with a knife, demanding my purse, a beautiful leather hand-carved purse Gran had given me for my birthday. Thankfully, I had been to the bank that afternoon and taken out $35 to buy groceries. Just as they opened my purse, a car drove out of Edgewater. Distracted, they looked up. I bolted as fast as I could run non-stop about a block and a half. They did not follow. I pounded on a neighbor's door and called the police.

The next morning two policemen arrived at my Newton Street townhouse, asking if I would come downtown to look at mug shots, which I did, of course. I have access to a photographic memory on and off, but always in crisis. I recalled the navy blue Pontiac with black Landau top, the fabric in their black slacks and jeans, their hats, what their shirts and jackets looked like, etc., etc. I discovered I had the dubious distinction of being the first person in history to ever be robbed at gunpoint in Madison Park.

Next, they waited in an alley on Magnolia for someone to bring out the Wednesday night trash. They jumped an elderly resident and beat him so badly he was in Harborview unconscious. He was the father of a Seattle policeman. With my description of the car, the Tacoma Police picked them both up in a gas station using my Shell Credit Card. They were both extradited to Georgia for two previous murders.

Another near-tragic event occurred when I was working Crisis Intake at Seattle Mental Health. We had federal money grant that was overseen by a Mr. Bose in Los Angeles. He came to Seattle for an Inspection Tour. My supervisor, asked me as a favor if I would go to dinner with Mr. Bose on Friday night. When Mr. Bose brought me home, he insisted on coming into to see my apartment. Before I knew it, he threw me on the guest bed in my second bedroom and jumped on top of me! In great shape from playing a lot of tennis, I threw him on his back on the floor! Mr. Bose said to me, looking up at me from the floor, "How can you deny yourself this opportunity?" Yuck!

dee McQuesten and Dog Alice; Madison Park Apartment… 1977

dee's new kitten, Mazel tov, adopted Dog Alice as
his Mother; Alice would have none of it!

CHAPTER EIGHT

Second Try

My search for home and family and belonging seemed to find resolution when after 12 years single, I married again – a man referred to (Prior to Bill Gates) as Seattle's "Most Eligible Bachelor," Leigh Shipman Davidson. Leigh charmed my sox off. He was lively; the best white man I ever danced with and, biggest bonus, a great tennis player. We played a lot of mixed doubles. His serve was in excess of 120 miles per hour. I recall the afternoon I first saw Leigh play Mens' Singles. He tossed the ball up; when his racket hit the ball, it exploded into a million pieces.

After three years of dating, we married. Leigh was retired at 31 years of age; tremendously affluent. He usually picked me up from work. We would have an early supper at a restaurant, his apartment or mine. Through those three years our evenings usually ended by 7 or 8. Leigh had phone calls to make, bills to pay, parents or his brothers to visit, etc. I never thought a thing of it. I had some community responsibilities, lots of evening tennis games; a Catholic dog, and Jewish cat to take care of. I never questioned what he did the rest of the evening. I trusted him.

Leigh and I were married by Father Joe Kramis at St. Patrick's Church in Roanoake Park on Saturday, April 12, 1980. Twenty months later our precious Morgan Dowe Davidson arrived. Leigh found and leased a wonderful little home on 36th and Mercer Street just two weeks prior to the wedding day.

The Saturday before the wedding the five Davidson brothers moved my furniture and accoutrements, clothes, etc., to our new home, while I stayed my final single week with my Maid of Honor and her mother nearby on Shenandoah Drive. I spent a lot of time power spraying the outside of the little white shake home, painting the inside, including the cellar steps, and sewing curtains.

Unbeknownst to me, while I was painting the Mercer Street kitchen, the Davidson brothers moved my furniture to Mercer Street. They emptied out my bookshelves, my lifetime collection, including my 9 years of English textbooks, etc., hauled them all to the Good Will. I had expected to house them in the generous bookshelves on either side of our new fireplace. No one consulted me. No one asked if I wanted to keep any of those special books. . . all gone – my entire collection of books, with the exception of one Shakespeare book from Angelo Pelligrini's class and Gran's Portobello Road leather-bound book of Tennyson Poems and 12 books in an upstairs bedroom. Why these twelve books were salvaged remains a mystery. There was a tragic miscommunication somewhere down the line. Nonetheless, the generous Davidson 5 gave up their whole day to move my household of heavy furniture from 43rd and Newton to 36th and Mercer. I was grateful.

We lived in this wonderful little home until we moved to our own first home on Dorffel Drive 8 years later.

One of my strongest memories of Dorffel Drive was when Morgan had Chicken Pox. He lounged around the Family Room downstairs for a couple of weeks watching VCR tapes and television. A strange odor began to emanate from the Family Room. I checked several times, trying to discern the odor's origin. Luckily, finally, I walked in when Morgan was peeing on the corner of the carpet against the wall. I said, "Morgan, why are you peeing on the carpet?" "I have to, Mommy, because I am watching a movie"! He was 6 – 1987.

A truly beautiful sisal rug on our large family room floor was unable to be salvaged by D.A. Burns' rug shampooing crew from such skullduggery, so it had to be ripped out in total and replaced.

Leigh had a very generous spirit. He was Executive Vice President of ENI, the largest oil and gas tax shelter company in the world. One year, early in our dating years, Leigh bought a bright yellow Ford Pinto for me at the PONCHO Art Auction; then taught me to drive a stick shift. So successful, Leigh was able to retire from ENI at 31.

Unfortunately, a greedy underhanded broker cunningly seduced him into investing many millions into the London Futures Market. At 33, Leigh lost everything.

Two weeks before our wedding, Leigh confided that, though he had already paid for the wedding lunch at the Broadmoor Golf Club for 265 people and our honeymoon trip to Mexico, he had only $35 left in the world. He insisted I didn't need to marry him. He was now a poor man. I said: "Nonsense! I could care less about your money. I generate a decent living as a freelance paralegal. I can support us while you decide what to do next." We moved forward.

To many men, self-worth is dependent upon how much money they have. With this total loss of funds, Leigh's spirit seemed broken; never to recover. He was quiet and solemn for years. He rarely spoke to me during our married life, never had any interest in doing anything together; never a walk or a movie; nothing. And no conversation. Twice a year he included me when he went to Dick and Jonna Jensen's for dinner. And twice a year we went to David and Linda Wyman's. Occasionally the Davidson's had family parties where I was included. That was it. Every year his mother, Sugar Davidson, (whom, I believe, paid for it), Morgan, Leigh and I dined out on my birthday.

Every Tuesday and Thursday night, when his best friend was in town, Leigh spent at the Mens' University Club having dinner and drinks until the wee hours. All day Sunday, every Sunday, starting in the early morning, until late evening, Leigh was gone with his best friend. I took it personally and found it very hurtful. Of course, I was thrilled at the time I could spend with Morgan, but felt I was married all by myself. Over the course of 14 years Leigh rarely spoke to me except to criticize me for one thing or another. I asked him if for every three criticisms if he could think of one nice thing to say, but that didn't interest him. It was not his style of communication. In public he had a totally different personality....one of affability, pleasantries and endless small talk.

I longed for some time the three of us could spend together as a family. It was not to be. The wound cut deeper and deeper as this pattern recurred month after month, year after year for 14 years.

It was an empty non-marriage, except, happily, for my dear little Morgan.

McQuesten-Davidson Wedding Day; Broadmoor Golf Club Luncheon Reception post-wedding ceremony at St. Patrick's Catholic Church; dee McQuesten, Gran McQuesten and dee's sister, Emily McQuesten...April 12, 1980

*dee wore Gran's hand-made Flapper Gown
on many special occasions...1991*

CHAPTER NINE

Morgan: At Last, a Child

By March, I was pregnant and in yet another conundrum about a marriage, quite lonely and lacking adult companionship. Leigh was very upset that I was pregnant, saying he wasn't ready for children. He soon acquiesced, however, and took me to the pre-natal classes at Swedish Hospital that very hot summer of 1981. We sat on floor mats. Pre-birth preparation was the most time we ever spent together. Sitting in the back row, I leaned back against the back wall and slept through most of the classes. Leigh was wide awake and fascinated. He absorbed each class conscientiously. The temperature rose to 108 degrees that August. Pregnant, my temperature was 20 degrees higher than normal; I was in full-time wilt mode!

I was working full time, however, as a freelance litigation paralegal for 54 law firms on call. I worked until 10 days before Morgan was born. Leigh still had no income.

On Sunday, December 20, 1981, after 48 1/2 hours of labor, Morgan Dowe Davidson arrived with a squeal; the most beautiful child I had ever seen! (Of course) I had a private corner room at Swedish. My nurse opened the drapes for me. It was 8:00 p.m., snowing on the lit spires of St James Cathedral. It looked like a Christmas card sent just to me, God saying:

"Merry Christmas, dee, Love, God." (Little did I know that 16 years later Morgan would be regularly ensconced in that same St. James Cathedral's little Mary Chapel prior to each game with his O'Dea football teams, for 20 plus years and likely forever.)

I was melting into happy tears, at 40 years old - the happiest woman on earth. The only sad thing was that Gran died the previous Sunday, so I couldn't take Morgan home. It was heartbreaking. My only consolation was I knew she Graduated and moved on to Heaven.

My doctor wouldn't let me fly home for Gran's funeral because it was too close to my "due date"...nor would he let me drive home because the passes were dangerously filled with steep snow. I missed Gran's funeral at Keith and Keith Funeral Home in Yakima, which was painful.

On Thursday, December 17, Royal Keith (our longtime family friend from Rimrock and Yakima) transported Gran's pale pink shimmerey casket over Snoqualmie Pass in a long black hearse as she was to be entombed in the Tacoma Mausoleum with Grandpa. My Brother, Joey, came, also. I fixed a noon meal for Joey, Morgan, Leigh and I before we traveled to Tacoma for our final good-byes.

Through the kitchen window, I saw Susan Jobs drive up to the front curb. I watched her ascend the front walk to the porch with a beautiful pink African Violet plant in hand. When she arrived at the front door, she said, "I wanted to give you a hug. I know how important your Gran was." (Susan, a trusted confidante, was the only person I ever confided in about Terry's domestic violence.)

That was Thursday, December 17. The next day, Friday, I began labor.

Morgan was a cheerful child, who never went through "the terrible two's". The best job I ever had was being Morgan's full time mother. I remain forever grateful for the opportunity. A million, zillion stories flow from my motherhood. I so wanted to be the mother Gran had been; so wanted to escape from the wounds of my birth mom. The challenge was ever before me – fear of failure; hope the love received in my early life and many summers thereafter would suffice to fortify me; teach me what love looked like for my own child. How I missed Gran's calm demeanor, her warm, soft voice.

The day after the long birthing process, my nurse told me Morgan was doing fine, with one exception. She had raised 5 children and had been a maternity nurse at Swedish for 35 years. She had never met a child as demanding as Morgan. She thought I should have some forewarning. Really? My precious tiny baby? How could that be? Little did I know what was ahead of me! Morgan developed quickly into a whirling dervish. Doctor Spector told me: "Not to worry. If a boy isn't in high gear as a child, he wouldn't be worth a nickel as an adult. So get used to it and be happy about it."

We brought Morgan home from the hospital on Christmas Eve. Within a half-an-hour I realized he'd need a clean diaper. In anticipation, I had been to Frederick & Nelson's, having noticed a diaper sale. I bought three packages of King-sized diapers. After a few moments of my struggle to put on a new diaper, the doorbell rang – Scott Wilson, a friend who had raised four children, was in town for a few days and just happened to pop by. I begged assistance in my first diaper change. He initially roared in laughter; King-Sized Diapers, he then pointed out, "were for 2 or three-year-olds". I bought large, thinking Morgan would grow into them. I dispatched Leigh to the grocery for some infant diapers!

Newly diapered, we placed Morgan under the Christmas Tree in a little Gerry Seat. Alice parked herself right next to him, having carefully sniffed around him and finding him, her first baby, acceptable. They became inseparable over the next several years, Alice always by his side until he began to chew on her ears. At that point, they parted ways for a time, 'til I was able to persuade Morgan that such chewing was inadvisable. Unable to pronounce "Alice," Morgan called her Lala which became her name from that point on.

It wasn't just Lala's ears; Morgan chewed anything he could reach. One morning, when I thought he was sleeping peacefully in our big king-sized bed while I worked at my desk, Morgan chewed the lace cuff across the entire width of the top sheet. That Christmas, while cooking dinner, I became aware that Morgan was particularly quiet. Dashing into the living room to check, I discovered the paint off all of the red balls on a full third of the Christmas tree – everything he could reach. He had sparkly red paint all over his face and down the front of his onesies!

Our neighbors near our little home on 36th and Mercer were remarkable. Andy, Marianna Price and their three boys lived across the street from us. Morgan's first social invitation (other than going to Aunt Frannie's on Christmas Eve when he arrived home from the hospital at 5 days old) was from Andy and Marianna. The snow was fairly deep. Andy and Marianna invited Morgan and myself for afternoon tea when Morgan was one month old. We bundled up warmly. Andy arrived at the front door to escort us down our two steps and safely across the icy street and up their steep steps to their home on the northwest corner of 36th and Mercer. We unbundled and settled into their sun room and BAM! Morgan began to scream at the top of his lungs, not yet ready to socialize. We three adults fussed and fussed, but could not convince him to cease screaming. After 20 minutes, Andy escorted us safely across the snow back to our front door. I discovered that Morgan was hungry

– a more experienced mother would have taken a warm bottle with us, but I had little clue about this new role!

Our other neighbors were vigilant and watchful over Morgan those first few tender years. One day Steve Rohrbach, across the street, was mowing their parking strip, when Morgan saw him then ran as fast as his little legs could move him up and down our parking strip and calling to Steve between the parked cars, ""Hi, Teve" for the whole 20 minutes Steve was working the strip. Morgan repeated that pattern each Saturday as long as we lived on Mercer Street. He loved "Teve".

Doctor Stu DuPen, (the anesthesiologist who stood vigilantly by my Swedish bed for the 48 ½ hours of labor), Carolyn, Siri (Morgan's first baby sitter) and brother John lived next door east. John and Morgan had a particularly good relationship. Morgan stood on Gran's hallway settee while John talked to Morgan through the front hall window. John was a terrific baby sitter. Morgan loved him.

There were other neighbors we treasured. The Tousley's around the corner, Andy and Marianna Price, Trina Jensen, the Griffin's, the Baugh's, Lee and Stu Rolfe, Ian Davis and, of course, the Rohrbachs. It was a wonderful block for Morgan to begin his life adventure.

Baby Morgan's favorite person when he was small was his Godmother, Linda Wyman. The minute he heard her voice, he came sliding down the old wooden stairs on the seat of his diapered pants. He adored Auntie Linda! His other favorite was Linda's husband, his Godfather, David E. Wyman. Uncle David carried him around on his shoulders, took him to the Puyallup Fair, and even showed up by surprise one Sunday afternoon, tossed Morgan on his shoulders and took him to his first baseball game – the Yankees against the Mariners. Every Thursday afternoon at 4:00, Uncle David telephoned to see how Morgan was doing. He spoke to

Morgan for a few minutes. Morgan thought it was a very big deal to get that phone call every week. Uncle David reminded him to be a good boy and to be sure to eat his vegetables!

As that first nurse predicted Morgan was always a delightful challenge. Once, introducing a new food to Morgan -- a spoonful of warm carrots – SPLAT!!! He spit them so far across the kitchen, about 8 feet, they stuck to the front of the stove. He liked squash better. And pears and peaches. Anything but carrots.

One evening when Morgan was twelve months old, Leigh and I were sitting at the kitchen table reading the paper, while Morgan sat on the two kitchen steps. Suddenly Morgan stood up, took three steps, stopped and clapped enthusiastically for himself, squealing with glee. He could walk. He was so proud; so were we!

One warm summer night I made a half gallon of purple grape Cool-Aid. Morgan sat at the kitchen table watching me give Alice a flea bath in the sink. After spending an hour washing, brushing and drying Alice with the hair dryer, I took the dryer back upstairs to the bathroom. Hearing a joyful shriek, I ran down the stairs. Morgan had dumped the whole half gallon of purple Cool-Aid on Alice! I called Leigh in the Tennis Club bar and said, "Please come home and take care of **<u>YOUR</u>** son, while I give Alice another bath."

Morgan offered me no end of surprising adventures. I once heard gleeful squeals coming from the kitchen at 2:00 a.m in the morning. I ran downstairs to find Morgan near an open refrigerator door, pulling the eggs out of their carton, squealing **"EGGGGEEEES!"** while dropping them on the floor. His cousin, Peter Davidson, had taught Morgan the game of "Eggies," in which he obviously found delight!

Morgan loved music. When he had a hard time going to sleep at night, I sang lullabies and other songs until he drifted off. Sometimes I rocked him to sleep. His favorite song was "Summertime." I remember with a smile the night I stood by his crib and sang "Summertime" for an hour and a half until he finally nodded off.

Another of Morgan's favorite things was a story (or two!) at bedtime. He had a Children's book, "Rags," about a huge English Sheep dog who guarded his family's grocery store by sitting on the counter next to the cash register. Morgan seemed to like this story. I read it several times, night after night. One night he burst into tears; his little cheeks turned bright red and his huge intense blue eyes were flashing. He said: "Mommy, PLEEEEEZE don't read that book again!" I said "Sweetheart, I thought this was your favorite book!" "No, Mommy. It's YOUR favorite book"! We put "Rags" away for a while. I still have it. It *was* my favorite!

When Morgan was three, he took up dusting. One evening, while I was on the phone with Kayla Skinner, sorting out Cornish Board items, Morgan was busy at his dusting projects; Kayla told Morgan that if he came to her house to dust, she'd give him Tuesdays off to go to the country!

On Morgan's third Halloween, while we were driving home from a childrens' party at Jonna and Dickey's home, Morgan said: "Daddy, did you marry Mommy?" "Why, yes I did, Morgan." "Oh, DARN! I was going to marry her,"!

As with many children, Christmas became more and more fun as Morgan grew. One particular Christmas, I wanted to give him a little red tricycle. I bought a kit. I sat up the whole night, until 4 in the morning putting it together, but it was missing two strategic bolts to stabilize it – no luck. Finally, I gave up and went to bed at 4 o'clock. At 4:30 Morgan bounced out of bed: "It's Christmas, Mommy, it's Christmas, did Santa come?"

On Morgan's 2nd Christmas, Grama Sug gave him a Mickey Mouse Watch. The day after Christmas I saw Morgan toss it into the garbage under the sink. I asked why he threw it away. Morgan said with firm conviction, "Me no like." To this day Morgan does not wear a watch. He meant it!

Leigh had dinner with us at the kitchen table only twice in 14 years. One evening, while Morgan and I sat alone at the dinner table, as we always did. Leigh was in the kitchen. Morgan said, echoing an emptiness I consistently felt but in his innocent child-like way: "Daddy, if you will eat dinner tonight with the Mommy and the Children, I will let you wear your tennis shoes to bed."

In our favorite white stucco Matsumoto-designed home at 275 Dorffel Drive in Denny Blaine, while setting up an office in our unfinished lower level, I discovered mice. I went to Lola's Madison Park Hardware to see about traps. She sold me some glue trays that had a dab of peanut butter on them. The idea was the mice would smell the peanut butter and get stuck in the glue. Unfortunately, our dog, Alice, smelled it first. Morgan was sick with the chicken pox. The Pacific NW Bell telephone lady had just arrived to hook up my office phone. Sick child, screaming dog, telephone lady – all at once. The kind phone lady offered to look after Morgan, who was watching movies in the family room, while I dealt with the dog. I wrapped up Alice in a towel, still stuck in the glue tray with all four paws, rushing her down to Doc Pearce at the Madison Park Veterinary Clinic. To my amazement and lasting offense, Dr. Pearce said: "Mrs. Davidson, I don't believe you have an appointment." I replied: "I rarely arrange emergencies by appointment!" He said he was sorry. He couldn't help us. I put Lala on the passenger seat, firmly wrapped in a towel, and held her down with my right hand as I drove with my left to a dog washing parlor on Eastlake. "Sure enough," she said. "I can clean the glue off Alice." Two hours later, telephone installed, child resting and myself slightly calmed, I picked up a washed and fluffed happy pooch.

For Morgan's 5th Birthday celebration, we took him and a classmate from his Bertschi School, to the Paramount Theater to see "Peter Pan." When Wendy swung out over the audience, his friend Alexander said, "Hey, Morgan, when Christmas is over, let's you and me take flying lessons!" They could not see the nylon ropes that supported Wendy. I spent the next three years watching Morgan carefully, as he wanted to jump off our second floor circular veranda off the living room, dining room and kitchen, to see if he could fly. Once, when Morgan and I were driving past Husky Stadium, he kept asking and asking if he could jump off the second floor terrace to see if he could fly. I had said "no" several times before. He insisted on an explanation. Finally, exasperated, I said, "Because it says so in the Parent Handbook!" Morgan started to cry, saying "Oh, that's no fair! Everyone knows adults don't understand children!"

He was growing up, my little boy. On our way to school, about 4 blocks from Mertschi, Morgan said: "Mommy, could you please pull over here and kiss me good-bye, instead of at school in front of the boys?"

Speaking of schools, the one thing Leigh and I agreed upon was to enroll Morgan in McGilvra Elementary, (Leigh's alma mater) our neighborhood school. However, with mandatory bussing rules, The Seattle School District rejected Morgan's application for McGilvra, enrolling him, instead, in a school far, far out in the south end. We decided to enroll Morgan in a private or parochial school nearby, which would fit my work schedule better.

At that point, Leigh's best friend took over! Although Epiphany School, short blocks from our home, had a long waiting list, the

Chairman of the Board called to ASK if they could have Morgan. I was astonished, knowing there was enormous competition to get in. I hoped for Morgan to attend a school nearby so he would have children in the neighborhood to play with. A private school, miles away, was certainly not the "neighborhood school" experience i hoped for Morgan.   Leigh's friend wanted Morgan to attend this school, so my opinion was inconvenient and irrelevant.

Mertschi was a miserable experience for Morgan. The children were mean. The parents meaner. Morgan was stuck there for 8 years, while I was forced to pay the enormous tuition, an indentured servant to Leigh and his best friend, unable to protect my dear little boy. These became the worst 8 years of Morgan's life, and of mine, as I watched it play out. The saving grace was he had three teachers who were fabulous: Ann Echols, Sara Carrasco and Leann, his third grade teacher. Teachers aside, Mertschi was a deep and horrifically expensive well of pain.

Lighter Notes

On a "Mom's break" trip to San Francisco, I found a wonderful stuffed, good looking rabbit for Morgan at I. Magnin. Morgan was just six. I took it home for him. We named him "Rags." One afternoon when Morgan was playing in and around the kitchen in our Dorffel Drive home, he tripped over Rags on the floor and split his chin wide open. I rushed him up to Swedish, as it was too far to Children's' Hospital for the amount of blood he was gushing. I was doing okay until I saw the 12" anesthetic needle moving toward his chin for stitches. After one quick glance at the needle. I fainted, . . .tough mom!

The widow who lived next door on Dorffel Drive, Renee Solomon, a transfer from Manhattan, had been, when younger, Jessica Tandy's schoolmate. Morgan was her biggest fan. Each day when I brought him home from school, he raced over to her home for a cookie. One day Morgan decided he should do something nice for her. On a sunny afternoon, he asked me to go over to the park with him across Dorffel Drive, since he was not allowed to cross the street alone. Morgan carefully picked hundreds and hundreds of bright yellow Dandelions, and shaped them into the largest bouquet I have ever seen! We walked over to Mrs. Solomon's. I rang the doorbell, Morgan's tiny hands occupied, barely holding up his enormous bundle. Mrs. Solomon was thrilled! She said, "Why Morgan, this is the nicest gift anyone has ever given me!" I believe she meant that, as she could see how much work it was for Morgan to pick such a huge bouquet of yellow flowers and then to lug them across the street and up Mrs. Solomon's stairs and sidewalk. It was a herculean effort on Morgan's part, which did not go un-noticed. I offered to help him carry part of his gigantic bundle, but he wanted to carry his flowers to Mrs. Solomon himself.

When we moved over to Dorffell Drive, dear Lala got old. She wandered out of her doggy door down the steps into the middle of the street and stood there. She had lost a lot of her sight and almost all her hearing and was regularly embarrassing herself on the living room carpet. Finally, when she was about 18 or 19, the sad day came. I fixed her a lovely meal the day after Thanksgiving – hot turkey, gravy, stuffing and pumpkin pie. Leigh took her to Doc Kramer's at the Capitol Hill Animal Clinic to put her to sleep. I didn't go. I couldn't. When Morgan got home from school, I explained that Lala was very old and she had peacefully fallen asleep. He was absolutely distraught! He invited all the boys in his class at Mertschi who had been to the house and played with Lala to come home after school that week for a funeral. I baked cookies. We had some juice and the boys all sat around and talked about what a good dog she was and how much they loved her.

I cried off and on for about a year. I missed that little yellow and white dog, soooo good natured and such an integral part of our family. One morning on the way to school, I started to cry again. Morgan said: "What's wrong, Mommy?" I said: "I miss Lala so much." Morgan said, "That's okay, Mommy. You can kiss me good-bye at school in front of the boys. I love you, Mommy."

(Twenty years later, I asked my theologically-educated husband if we get our pets back when we get to Heaven. Paddy, scratching his chin, head tilted, replied, "deedeemac, I don't know for certain if we get our pets back. What I *Do* know for sure is if we are *very* good on earth, we get all our sox back!")

Leigh promised Morgan he could have another dog soon. But, right then, Morgan had to compromise with Dad for a gold fish. Morgan and I found one in a pet shop on Capitol Hill. We bought a bowl and some food. That worked for about a week until one morning before school we found the poor fish floating on top of the water. Oh dear. I bought another one. Same thing. The second time Morgan was completely beside himself. He had to have a funeral immediately before going to school, now at St. Joseph's. I called Dad who met us at the empty roped-off parking lot of Dick's Hamburgers on Broadway. We had some prayers and a little funeral for Morgan's fish. Every time, for many years when visiting Dick's, I check for that same parking spot, while drinking my chocolate shake!

The subject turned to getting a new dog. Leigh said "Not yet." He said "Not Yet" for over two years. Morgan begged and pleaded. "Why not, Daddy?" Leigh was never ready and never would be ready. It felt cruel to make Morgan wait for what felt like an interminable time to a 6-year-old boy, 7-year-old boy, 8-year-old boy who missed his little dog. So, one spring morning, in 1989, two years after Lala died, on the way to school, I promised Morgan I would pick him up after school at the usual time.

We would go dog shopping. He could have any dog he wanted. He could pick the dog out himself. We went first to the King County Humane Society on 15th Avenue West. Morgan saw a Basset Hound he liked a little, but he wasn't sure. So, we traveled out to 85th to the Ridlow Pet Store. The clerk opened a cage with a litter of three puppies who came scampering out. Morgan sat on his haunches, playing with them. One, a tiny little yellow and white pup, jumped on Morgan's lap and pushed him over backwards, licking his face. With no lingering doubt, Morgan insisted: "I want this one, Mommy!" That was it. $90 for some food, a license and a King Charles Spaniel.

Leigh was enraged! He hollered that I did not have permission to buy Morgan a dog! For the next 6 weeks he sulked, not speaking to me. On one of the two occasions in 14 years that he sat at the dinner table with us, he kept it up: "Morgan, would you ask your mother to pass the salt?" Things grew from bad to worse.

Leigh had numerous leg surgeries, results of an auto accident long before we married. In the days before seat belts, a friend of his driving, crashed. Leigh's knees were crushed under the dashboard of the small sports car. After 2 surgeries Leigh's insurance was canceled. Once Morgan was in school, I worked 5 part-time jobs (simultaneously) to pay for the next 11 surgeries. I was determined to only commit to part-time work, as I wanted to take Morgan to school and be the one to pick him up. I did some P.R. work for the Mediterranean Womens' Store on Pine Street, a little P.R. for the Empty Space Theatre, two restaurants on Broadway, and sold residential water filters for Uncle Billy Davidson, while renovating two homes.

We loved our home on Dorffel Drive. However, I found myself burdened with financing Leigh's multiple knee surgeries, school tuition, mortgage, etc. To keep us out of bankruptcy, I had to sell Dorffel, purchase a home in Mt. Baker, renovate it; sell that one, too. The day Duncan and Sons finished packing up the truck, as we were about to leave the Dorffel house, Morgan said, "Oh, Mommy, can we put it all back? I don't want to move", nearly breaking my already fractured heart.

Two memorable Meals

While living at our Dorffel Drive home, Morgan realized he liked giving parties. One October, when Morgan was 7, we invited 40 people for dinner, to celebrate his dad's birthday Morgan loved to help cook and bake, standing on his kitchen stool to reach up to counters and sinks.

We made a list with Dad, called everyone. Morgan and I cooked and baked for 5 days with enthusiastic anticipation for Dad's upcoming Saturday birthday dinner.

On Friday night Leigh said, his best friend had David's Lear Jet, pilot and co-pilot for the weekend. His best friend did not wish to attend Leigh's birthday dinner at our home. "He wants us to celebrate my birthday at the Pacific Union Club in San Francisco, so I can't make the party here at home tomorrow night!"

I can still hear Morgan's tiny little 7-year-old voice saying, "Why, Daddy? Why can't you come to your Birthday Party? but we have already cooked the food". Morgan was just as devastated as I was. Morgan loved Dad. What hurt me the most was to see the pain of disappointment on his face. It was one thing to disappoint me. I was an adult. I couldn't comprehend how Leigh could do this to his 7-year-old child. I didn't really know my husband. I had no idea what made him tick or who he was. Why was his best friend more important, more valuable, than his wife, his marriage, his family, or his son.

"We leave early tomorrow morning; I'll be home late Sunday night, maybe Monday. I know how hard you and Morgan have worked getting ready for my birthday dinner party, but this spontaneous trip is important to my best friend". 'Twas ever thus. Over and over and over, 'twas ever thus.

I was paralyzed with shock and disappointment. The table was already set for the buffet, with my good china and crystal, Gran's sterling dinner ware, linens were ironed and laid out, flowers on the table. It looked beautiful. Leigh stood in front of the elaborately-prepared buffet table in the dining room, where he made this announcement.

(I had a flashback to three months into my dating life with Leigh in 1977. One afternoon he called to say he would like to take me to the Seattle Yacht Club this coming Friday for dinner with his best friend. The purpose of the dinner was for his best friend to approve of me. I laughed, thinking he was JOKING!....The day after our dinner Leigh called to say I had passed the litmus tests – that I was officially "approved". Leigh could have a relationship with me; I wouldn't cause any trouble or stir the waters. I still thought he was joking. Why would his best friend have to approve of me?)

That evening, I was overcome with a lonely hollow feeling. 'Twas ever thus over and over and over. I had no vote, no voice, no value. I was invisible, inconvenient, again! Don't ask questions. Don't speak up. Just earn the money and pay the bills. I had no other value but to do the laundry, be responsible for the housework and grounds while Leigh lounged on the sofa watching TV, not working, surgery after surgery with his best friend's incompetent surgeon.

It was Terry all over again. It was my birth mother all over again.

Did I imagine the conversation? Did Leigh really say that, standing in front of the elaborately set dining room/flowered table, then fix himself a rum and Tab, pack his bag for his three-day weekend and walk downstairs to the family room to watch TV for the rest of the night? While Morgan and I sat upstairs at the kitchen table, having dinner alone? Did he really say that? I was numb. It was ever the same answer.

It didn't matter what the subject was, I was at once invisible and inconvenient. If I didn't dawn the mantle of invisibility, I was a nuisance; an inconvenience. My job was to earn the money, pay all of the bills, including the mounting hospital bills, be quiet, don't ask any questions. Just pay the bills.

When it was time to seek an insurance broker for our home, I was not allowed to participate in the research in locating one – or the final decision in choosing a broker. Leigh's best friend instructed him to insure our home with Parker, Smith and Feek. No questions allowed on my part. 2 months after we signed a contract with them, the main principal, Parker, retired, so we were without a personal contact again for insurance purposes.

Why was I working 5 part-time jobs to pay the mortgage, insurance, school tuition, groceries, car insurance and rapidly paying off $200,000.00 in hospital surgery bills, while Leigh went from leg and knee surgery to surgery to surgery, unable to work? I urged him (no, I BEGGED him) to get a second medical opinion, but this same best friend insisted he remain with this doctor –his friend's doctor – who performed all 13 surgeries. I was paying for the last 11 surgeries, as our insurance was cancelled after the first two. WHY? OH WHY? OH WHY was I doing this? I had no partner, no husband, no companion, no friend, no marriage, nothing. I found myself once again overcome with anxiety/knots in my stomach, internally paralyzed with emotional pain in the position of an indentured servant. I longed to be part of a marriage team, a family, but it was never going to happen. This marriage was between three people: Leigh, his best friend and least of all, me with no participation rights. Truly, Leigh had none, either. He did whatever his friend dictated. Made no sense to me, but it was frightening. As hard as I tried, I could never figure it out. Why was Leigh beholding to this man? It made no sense to me.

Two years after I divorced Leigh, someone in the Davidson family finally convinced him to get a second opinion - at the Polyclinic. He quickly discovered, what we could have known years and many surgeries earlier, that all his surgeries had been unnecessary; Leigh had Multiple Sclerosis, the source of numbness in his legs.

It would have helped if I could even have a good cry to dissolve the knots in my stomach, but my birth-mother had beaten that possibility out of me, constantly telling me "Good girls don't cry!" "Don't you DARE cry, or I'll give you something to cry about!" I could still hear her angry screaming in my ears: "Don't you **DARE** cry!" So I remained invisible and inconvenient – still – and again.

Years before computers/emails/texting/messaging, it was too late to reach 40 people. Some of Leigh's friends were coming in from out of town especially for his birthday. The fridge was full of wonderful entrée, salads and desserts. The only possibility was to proceed with the birthday party.

It was surreal, like I was standing in the middle of a Salvador Dali painting, taking my instructions from Franz Kafka, in 1988. This relationship was meaningless. Empty. Hopeless. I was married all by myself -- again. Why?

Morgan, at 7 years old, was the affable man of the house that Saturday night. The quintessentially perfect host. He opened the door, greeting everyone, offering hors d'oeuvres. We explained that Leigh was at the Pacific Union Club in San Francisco with his best friend. It fell flat, hollow. Everyone had puzzled looks on their faces, even Leigh's family -- "He's WHERE?" Some guests brought presents for Leigh, which we stacked in the corner of the dining room. Why was I surprised? This was how we lived. I was inconvenient. Leigh's best friend was convenient. I was not.

We did have one especially fun dinner party on Dorffel: Leigh and his best friend were traveling up to Campbell River to fish for salmon. Leigh asked me to invite a few people for a small dinner. It was near Kayla's, birthday, so I invited mutual friends to celebrate her.

We asked Joe McDonnel (Seattle's Premier, liveliest and most FUN Caterer, and owner of the renowned Seattle private Club, *The Ruins*) to cater dinner on a Saturday evening -- a nice salmon feast with the fish that Leigh would bring home from Canada.

Little did I know how absolutely thorough and aesthetic Joe was. He was an hysterically funny, wonderfully brilliant artistic dream. I had known Joe for over 10 years, but never before as one of his clients.

The production began on **Tuesday morning, 7:00 a.m.**: Joe appeared on my doorstep in his white apron, unannounced, (I in my jammies and robe) to take a look at my "set-up." He walked through the Dorffel house with his discerning eye, making decisions and helpful suggestions.

Wednesday morning, 7:00: Joe appeared on the front steps, again unannounced. He wanted to take another look at the dining room.

"Oh, dee Darling, what other OPTIONS do you have for a dining room table?"

My Grandmother's dining room table. I loved it. Was there some-thing wrong with it?

To which Joe insisted, "This simply won't do. It's a Duncan Fife! Can't we do something else? This beautiful dining room deserves a table with some flare. Isn't there ANYTHING else you can do? Don't you have something in storage? How about downstairs? Is there anything there we can use? This table has no pizazz. Surely you can think of SOMETHING!"

I talked to Leigh, who was somewhat baffled. He said, "My parents are in Hawaii for 2 more weeks. I suppose Mom wouldn't mind if we borrowed her dining room table if we were very careful."

So off we went through the Broadmoor gates in my station wag-on with blankets to capture Sugar Davidson's table. We carefully roped her beautiful walnut ornate table upside down on top of my wagon. Back out through the gates, across Madison Street and up to Dorffel Drive.

Thursday morning: There was Joe on my front steps at 6:45 a.m. Bright and cheery, as if he had been up for hours. Maybe he had! By now, realizing Joe was a morning person, I had my bathrobe on, teeth brushed, hair combed!

"dee Darling, I need to check your linens," Joe announced.

To which I replied, "My linens are great. I have a beautiful set of Irish chrysanthemum linens from Gran, washed, starched, and ironed just this week."

"Fine. I need to see them," Joe said.

I proudly retrieved them from the linen closet to show them off. Certainly they would meet his seal of approval. No such luck!

"The linens are fine, but where is your ironing board?" Joe proceeded to stand in my kitchen, in his white apron, re-ironing all eight dinner napkins with a different fold! All the while claiming with wild enthusiasm this was the best kitchen he had ever had for catering. He couldn't wait to cook in it - so accommodating.

Friday morning, ten minutes to 7:00: Joe on the front porch in his white apron, "dee, darling, I need to check your flowers for the table and the dining room chairs. Those Duncan Fife chairs aren't going to work. Options?"

"I have no options, Joe. These go with Gran's table – there are no other choices downstairs or in some magical storeroom."

"Well, never mind. I have the perfect chairs. I will bring them over in the morning. Put these away."

"Now, about your flowers?" "The flowers are done, Joe. I bought three bunches of freesias last night at Bert's. I love freesias; their color and their scent. Don't you?"

"dee Darling, these won't do at all….Don't worry about it…I will bring the center piece tomorrow."

Saturday Morning, 7:00: Joe on the front porch, white apron, cheery as can be, like he's been up for hours and having another super-fun day!

"dee Darling, we need to talk about your front steps."

"What's wrong with my front steps?" "When were they last swept?" "Day before yesterday when the gardener was here. They look clean to me. Is there something wrong?"

"Well, they're sort of okay. Where's your broom?"

We had a LOT of front steps from the door down to Dorffel Drive. And there was Joe in his white apron sweeping his heart out to the point that he deemed the steps perfect.

"You see, dee Darling, when you give a dinner party, it is a total experience from the time your guests step out of their car at the curb, up the steps, past the potted flowers (of which he DID approve) until dessert and brandy are over. There is much more to it than just the hors d'oeuvres, drinks, entrée and dessert. The aesthetics are an important part of the experience."

I hid the banished freesias on a table in the master bedroom.

Saturday Afternoon, 2:00: Joe appeared once again, with the ten most beautiful dining room chairs I have ever seen in my life -- French Louis IV, walnut with heart-shaped backs and gorgeous green velvet seats floating atop the ornate legs.

Joe also trundled up the stairs with a 2' long rectangular low pewter basket for the table, filled with green moss and short exquisite bright tiny flowers. A visual feast!

Joe did allow me to set the table, trusting I could manage it properly. I knew where each fork went and in what order, where the dessert spoon should be above the plate, etc. I did a good job. Joe was proud of me! I achieved at least a B-. He winked at me, so I knew I was doing okay.

Saturday Afternoon, 4:00: I had an emergency call from Leigh. They hadn't caught any salmon, after all at Campbell River. The fish weren't running, so I should figure out something else for dinner. It was 4:00!

I called Joe right away, who rushed to the Pike Place Market and picked up a beautiful salmon. He was only planning on doing hors d'oeuvres, soup, salad, and dessert. But he shifted into high gear immediately and made it all work.

Saturday Afternoon, 5:00: Joe showed up with his sous chef and crew and went to work.

Saturday Night, 7:00: Guests began to trickle up the perfectly swept sidewalk and front steps, past the perfectly potted pink and white impatience.

That was aesthetically the most beautiful and scrumptious meal and dining room I could imagine, like something out of <u>Architectural Digest</u> or <u>Town and Country</u>.

Sadly, Joe died way too young. What a treasure he was. To have known him, with his level of happy energy, his creativity and tremendous sense of humor was indeed a privilege; a spirit boost at every encounter. I miss him. Seattle misses him. And I miss Dorffel Drive. Morgan and I loved that home.

Mistaken Identity

One morning, while driving Morgan to St. Joe's Grade School, we stopped behind a car on Roy Street and 19th, heading west. We waited and waited for him to either move ahead or turn right. We waited and waited impatiently. I didn't want Morgan to be late for school.....this fumble-headed driver just SAT THERE!!! Finally, Morgan said, "Mommy, that's a parked car!"...sure enough!

I was fortunate to find Mary Roos who had a day-care in her home on Capitol Hill. She took wonderful care of Morgan during the summer and after school. Morgan loved her and was quite possessive, calling her always "**My** Mary," insisting on this title to the other children in Mary's home.

We have wonderful stories from his time with Mary Roos. One sunny afternoon, on the way home from "My Mary's," Morgan said, "Mommy, My Mary is sad today." "Why, Morgan?" "Mommy, do you know what an apartment is? An apartment is a house that lives on top of a house. MY Mary's son, Johnnie, is moving into one."

The next day it was "Guess what, Mommy? MY Mary's mailman came to bring some mail today with brown legs!" I said: "Sweetheart, what color legs do YOU have?" "MY Mary and I have silver legs!"

For Morgan's 7th Birthday, I drove his guests to Chucky Cheese in Tukwila on a snowy night. We were singing Christmas Carols. From far back in my old blue Mercury station wagon, I heard Jill Pasquale say, "Morgan, when we get big, will you marry me?" To which Morgan replied, "I **already TOLD YOU NO!"** I said, "Morgan, you had better think that one over. Jill's a reeeeeally nice girl; and she's good at math, art and everything else. Let's not be too hasty."

One afternoon in 1989, I had picked up Mike and Sky Sander for a play date at our home on Lake Washington Boulevard. The three boys, about seven, were sitting in the way back of my looooong blue and woody Mercury Station Wagon. They thought I couldn't hear them talking. Mike piped up: "Hey, Morgan, I found out what an affair is!" Morgan: "What?" Mike: "It's when someone's mom and someone else's dad meet secretly in the Produce Department at Bert's Grocery"!!!

Later Married Years

One stormy afternoon during Seattle's "Hundred Year Rainstorm," in the late 80's, our home began to slide. While I sat upstairs in the den, on the phone, I noticed the walls beginning to crack. I called Howie Wright, owner of Howard S. Wright Construction Co. He was in Los Angeles; his secretary paged him. Howie called back right away. Within 20 minutes he had people all over our hillside and yard, covering everything with black visqueen. The sliding stopped, thanks to Howie's quick response. But we were forced to move to the Lake Union Marriott Residence Hotel for three months while the house was renovated and fortified once more on the hillside. 30' deep soldier pile walls were driven in on two sides of the house to stabilize it before the construction began. Curiously, because our previous agent had retired, I had just switched our homeowners insurance to Safeco 48 hours earlier. Safeco was not amused!

The neighbor to our south revealed that he was not surprised when our home and the home next door slid because all three homes on our lane were built "on sin money," he said. The contractor who had built them lived next door to us. He grew and sold many thousands of dollars' worth of Marijuana in the basement of his home. When he was discovered, I watched him slide out quietly one night into a taxi to fly to Norway. I later heard was in prison in Norway for the same charge.

Shortly after the repairs to our house were completed, an exchange student, Atsufumi Miyata, came from Tokyo to live with us, to study English at the University of Washington – a great time for Morgan. They played tennis and soccer together. Atsufumi taught him to read, speak and write a little Japanese. We all had a wonderful year with him and his legion of friends, surely the best of our married life.

I enjoyed all Morgan's sports when he was growing up. He began with Montlake "T-ball." Morgan wasn't very interested in the game. He often sat down in the dirt near third base drawing pictures on the ground with a stick while his dad was hollering, "Morgan, heads up! Watch the ball!"

Morgan excelled at Water Polo at the Tennis Club. With very strong lungs, he outlasted the other team members. He loved Montlake Softball, soccer, St. Joe's basketball, St. Luke's basketball and ultimately, his real and lasting love, four years of football at O'Dea. Morgan also managed the O'Dea Varsity Basketball team his junior and senior years.

One summer, when Morgan was 11, I took him to New York vacation for the two of us. We had a wonderful 9 days in the city. With only a scant income, I sold some furniture to finance our trip. Morgan chose what he wanted to do. We followed his instincts. His first hope was to see the United Nations. He climbed to the top of the Statue of Liberty and visited the top of the Empire State Building. I had been told the view from the Windows on the World Restaurant in the Twin Towers, lost in 911, was spectacular, so we visited that restaurant early one afternoon.

Mardy and Bob Sander, Jane and the twins, Morgan's best friends, were in New York at the same time. We met them for dinner at Ken Griffey's restaurant and prowled around Times Square. We also had one dinner at Mickey Mantle's Baseball Restaurant.

When Morgan was in middle school began to physically grow and grow and grow. He grew 18" in 18 months. By the time he reached O'Dea, he was among the tallest men in his class. When he donned his football uniform and helmet, he became even more daunting. He was now enrolled in the school of his own choice and playing on his dream high school football team. It was 1996.

Coach Monte Kohler checked student's grades on Wednesdays. If your grades were not 2.3 or above, you were not allowed to suit up for the Friday night football game. Morgan missed only one time. I attended that game, as always, unknowing, expecting to see him play. There he was delivering water buckets in a jacket and slacks. Very different uniform! He never let that happen again.

One rainy November day, in 1990, the 45 degree long steep driveway from Lake Washington Boulevard down to our garage was so covered with thick slippery leaves that we could not drive up the hill. For three hours, I raked everything into a huge pile, then climbed up to the third floor Family Room, where Leigh and Morgan were watching TV. I asked Leigh to come down and help me by holding the large black plastic yard bags so I could push in all the leaves. Leigh, not moving from his couch, said: "If you can't handle the chores, we can move to an apartment," as he continued to watch TV for the rest of the day and night while I bundled the leaves. I had no value. I was inconvenient, except for the chores.

I underwent serious marriage counseling with four different marriage counselors — by myself. Leigh was not interested. He was happy with the status quo, he said, but "if counseling made me feel better about myself," he would support the idea of me going alone. I naively sought a counselor who could "fix it." No such magician existed. Finally, after 6 years of warning, I told Leigh I was leaving. I meant it. His honest and only reaction:

"But Who's Going to Do the Laundry"?

Tom Skerritt, TV and movie favorite, and Madison Park neighbor, and I met in the bowels of the Madison Park Hardware Store searching for furnace filters one morning. We became instant good pals. Howie Wright asked me to introduce him to Tom, an easy arrangement. Howie was interested in investing in local film making, utilizing his gifts and reputation to bolster the Seattle's economy.

I introduced them at a breakfast at the Madison Park Cafe. There began a good and fruitful friendship until Howie's sudden death of heart complications in surgery.

I also thought Colby Chester, among other things, a well-known local actor and friend, should meet Tom and also Stewart Stern (writer/producer of all James Dean's films). I took the three of them to lunch – up, up and away.....I love connecting people who need to know each other. They subsequently developed a film and screen writing school together. I added David Skinner into the mix, as David was interested in getting involved in the film industry. Together, they founded "Shadow Catchers".

One afternoon the kitchen phone rang about 2:00. It was Tom. Tom, with loooong drawn out easy droll speech, "Hi, dee. This is Tom; I'm in Montana shooting 'The River Runs Through it' feature film. I need you to chair the Opening Premier Gala for the movie." He wanted it to be a dual benefit for his son Colin's Northwest School and Robert Redford's favorite cause, the Elwah Dam. I told him that I was overwhelmed with activities at school for Morgan, working several part-time jobs to pay Leigh's hospital bills and some other things. It wasn't possible!

To which Tom answered, "Just a minute. Bob wants to talk to you." I had no clue who "Bob" was . . . but there he was. Robert Redford, explaining to me the importance of this gala to the Elwah River Dam, etc., asking me to chair the benefit. It's very difficult to say no to "Bob", so there I was, in charge of the whole schlemeel, like it or not. We had a grand time; made a little money and the film was off and running, becoming an all-time classic!

To begin my gradual escape from a second failed marriage while assuring the least possible trauma to my dear Morgan, I moved up to Tom Skerritt's home on Capitol Hill during the week, while

Tom was filming "Picket Fences," in Hollywood. I went home each morning to fix Morgan breakfast and get him to school. I spent the afternoon with him doing homework, driving him to his sports, etc. After dinner, when I had tucked Morgan in, I returned to Tom's for a couple of hours of solitude and to think things through, perhaps an hour or two of sleep.

Again my search for a home, a place to belong, the warm familiarity of Rimrock and Yakima had escaped me; my second marriage failed.

Morgan and I picked out an apartment in Madison Park. We began the next chapter of our lives.

Again, an inconvenient wife, no longer.

*Grama "Sug" Davidson and Grandfather Bill Davidson
with one-month-old Morgan...January, 1982*

Morgan Dowe Davidson's Baptism; Father Marlin Connole,
Morgan, Leigh and dee McQuesten-Davidson...June, 1982

Baby Morgan Dowe Davidson...1982

Morgan was afraid of Santa when she was one;
Nordstrom's downtown window…December, 1982

Morgan was less afraid of Santa when he was two…1983

Morgan with dee in Gran McQuesten's Flapper Gown ...1984

*Morgan riding Uncle Billy Davidson's Rocking
Horse in the Nursery...1985*

Morgan's cowboy boots – Size 3 – Gift from Christopher Laughlin

Morgan wading at Madrona Beach…1985

Morgan's first trip to Disneyland...Leigh Davidson,
Morgan pulling Goofy's nose

Morgan's First Fish….EEEEUUUWWW!!!…Medina Pond…1985

Photo by Aunt Sally Davidson

Mothers' day, 1989...Sign says: "My Mom is the best Mom in the world because she bought me the best dog in the world."

*One sunny Saturday afternoon, during the short time we
lived in the Mt. Baker neighborhood, Morgan's Godfather,
David E. Wyman, taught Morgan how to prune roses!*

Morgan's dog, Rasky (Iraskin from "Crocodile Dundee")
liked to lick his hair after a shower...1989

Morgan rocking on the Veranda of the Ala Moana
Hotel on Kalakaua Avenue...Oahu...1989

Morgan and Mom on Christmas Day, 1989...Honolulu

Morgan with new puppy, Rasky…1989

Morgan and Mom in Jeans...1987

Rasky always wore a bow tie on Christmas…every night she insisted on ¾ of Morgan's pillow….she only allowed him a small corner…1987

Sky Sander, Mike Sander, Morgan...Ken Griffey
Restaurant...Time Square, New York City...1993

Morgan's O'dea Graduation....June, 2000

Morgan's 21st Birthday...December 20, 2001

dee's 54ᵗʰ Birthday with Morgan at Canlis
Restaurant…a gift from Alice Canlis

Morgan's 21st Birthday...Patrick Jaikka, Guest Artist, dee, Pat Carroll

Morgan, having a brilliant sense of humor, surprised a Golden Retriever

Morgan played football for O'dea Catholic Mens'High School
for four years...1996-2000...with Mom on Senior Night

Morgan at Mom and Stepfather, Pat Carroll's, mutual
birthday celebration...August 10, 2006

CHAPTER TEN

Civic Engagement

Over the years I have consistently involved myself with the world I live in, in projects large and small, trying to help out as best I can. My grandfather spent most of his 9 decades as a public servant; growing up in that milieu formed me. I suspect my birth-mother's narcissistic total self-absorption also influenced my need to reach out beyond myself, to live, at least in part, for others; not just myself. I have already mentioned my work on the "Save the Market". There have been many more such involvements.

A few months after my wedding to Leigh Davidson, ensconced as I was and am in Madison Park, I decided Madison Park, with all its history and activity, should have a neighborhood newspaper. I founded, edited and published a paper that still exists, The Madison Park Post (now "Madison Park Times"). The first issue was December 12, 1980. When I mentioned the idea to my sister-in-law, Sally Davidson, she made the mistake of saying, "You can't do that. You don't have the money to begin such an undertaking and you have no journalism experience." No one should ever tell me I can't do something. The neighborhood owes Sally gratitude for challenging me.

There was a small closet in what would become the nursery up-stairs in our small home on 36th and Mercer, with a single light bulb hanging by a string. There I sat and typed the stories, which I wrote; I took all the photos and I laid out the paper on our din-ing room table. King TV showed up one Sunday afternoon, com-pletely unannounced, to film what became a feature story on my entrepreneurship, closet, light bulb, electric typewriter, primitive printer and all.

The paper came out once a month, at which time I delivered it door-to-door throughout Broadmoor, Washington Park and Madison Park, rain, shine or snow, until Carol Jacobson began sell-ing subscriptions, which were annual.... It was $ 12.00 for one year to have the paper mailed to your door. Otherwise, the papers were free at Bert's, Madison Park Hardware and a few other places. The ads I sold paid for the paper.

I set the paper up as a non-profit with a neighborhood board of Jim Allison, Dick Clark, Carol Jacobson and Bobby Arnold to give me ideas for stories. Rabbi Starr from Temple de Hirsch wrote a sports column. After two successful years, David Brewster, already publishing *The Weekly*, wanted to buy the pa-per. I told David I would sell it for $1200. His Financial Manager for the "Seattle Weekly," Mike Crystal, insisted no. They could not manage two papers. Eventually, I simply gave the paper to Murray Publishing, which had several neighborhood papers al-ready, with the promise they would continue it as a Madison Park newspaper. Asking only that they keep it going, I turned over all my advertisers, contacts, phone numbers, etc. The pa-per continues and thrives to this day. Murray Publishing changed the name to "Madison Park Times".

Washington Park Christmas Tea (and Eggnog) Party

Sarah Baugh and I originated the "Washington Park Christmas Tea," in 1983 – An event at which everyone brought food to stock up local food banks for the holidays; a ton of food was always donated. We had our first tea, for 350 women, at our home on Mercer Street. It was a lovely event. Fortunately, it did not rain that day, as people were parked clear down to Madison Street. This day, I served hundreds of home-made cookies and breads, vegetables and my infamous egg nog. Several people loved the nog so much, they had to walk home! I had baked all the treats myself, little Morgan standing by for two weeks, while this happened, offering help, while consuming cookie dough and goodies. He was two. I hosted the second Tea at our Boulevard House; another 350 mostly women. The third one at Edgewater and a more recent one at Washington Park Tower. The Washington Park Christmas Tea continues successfully to this day.

There were at least 50 treats left the morning after that first 1983 Tea. Morgan and I put them all in a very large box and took them to his Pediatrician, Gary Spector. We arrived at Doctor Spector's office, Morgan in his small navy blue pea coat and red Muppet hat. Morgan walked into his waiting room, carrying an enormous box, about 14" x 14" and heavy. Just then Gary walked through his lobby. Morgan said, "Mairdy Krimmus, Dokker Gairdy." The cookies, but more than that, Morgan, made a big hit!

As part of my engagement, I always stayed close to Morgan's school activities. For Bertschi, I chaired the Corporate Procurement for their auction. At St. Joe's I co-chaired a major "Artist in Residence" project, engaging a Native American carver to carve a totem pole for the school. At O'Dea I attended all of the Mothers' Club meetings, took on the role of

Historian and several other challenges, including entertainment for a Scholarship Luncheon.

Not all community endeavors have resulted in financial wellbeing on one level or another. We had equality/gender discrimination problems at the Tennis Club. I joined the Seattle Tennis Club as a Junior Member. I have been appreciatively active for tennis, squash, swimming and canoeing for almost 60 years. One Saturday morning in 1980 Marianne Lorenz and I were playing singles on Court Two. In the middle of my serve in the first set, two rude men (whom I shall not name,) walked onto our court, saying: "Alright, girls, you have had enough fun!" Infuriated with the rules that male members of the club had 100% right to all the courts every weekday from 3:00 on and most of Saturdays and Sundays, Marianne and I contacted a member attorney, who politely explained to the Board that, as a non-profit, it was illegal to discriminate. If the Board did not amend the rules immediately, giving equal access to the courts to the women members, she would have no choice but to report the discretion to the Washington State Liquor Board, eliminating the club's liquor license! The Board changed the rules instantly!

Raising money for non-profits endures as a central commitment to myself. As a Trustee of Cornish College of the Arts for ten years, I donated approximately 14,000 hours in ten years' time and raised money for scholarships and annual operation costs. I brought on 16 members to the Cornish Board; many of whom are still there.

After I had been on my own for a couple of months following my divorce from Leigh, Bruce Hunter, Principal of Washington Middle School, called me for a favor. He had 42 homeless students that his bus picked up each morning from the shelters. This week it was 14 degrees. He had kids with holes in their shoes, no sox, inadequate jackets, shirts, pants too short, no hats, scarves, underwear or gloves. He asked if I could help. I thought of a good friend who owned a clothing store. I visited him in his office, explaining Mr. Hunter's predicament. Without any hesitation, handed me his credit card and said, "Get their sizes and take this to the store and get whatever the students need." Just like that! What a wonderful, incredible human being!

I made arrangement with the Washington Middle School Nurse for sizing. No one, even the teachers at school, knew which students were homeless, except the school nurse. She later confided that during her sizing, one little boy said to her, "Do all of the students get new clothes for Christmas?" She had replied, "No, Jimmy. Only the special ones."

A week later, one of the teachers invited me to their class Christmas party. The teacher introduced me to one of the parents of a homeless child and said, "Jimmy's father would like to thank you." I replied, "Don't thank me. The new clothes are compliments of one store owner. He has a very big heart and outfitted all 42 kids."

Jimmy's Dad said, "Is there any way I can thank him?" I said, "I think so, if he is in his office. I have the number on his desk." I immediately dialed from the teacher's phone. Fortunately, he answered the phone; Jimmy's Dad began to tearfully thank him. As he handed the phone back to me. The store owner said to me, "dee, this phone call made my whole Christmas!"

One downside to this story: The manager of the store called me three days later to ask if he should accept returns on the clothes and shoes from a couple of parents who wanted to trade them in for cash. I said absolutely not!!!

Morgan's Christmas Gift

I'm grateful my commitment to helping others seemed to be contagious, even early on: While Morgan and I were dashing in and out of Washington Middle School one VERY cold winter, delivering new clothes and shoes, the week before Christmas a teacher invited us into the "Special Ed" classroom.

A student, Isaiah, 13, unable to speak, confined to a wheelchair in a head and neck brace was suffering from severe Cerebral Palsy. The Special Ed Teacher informed us that Isaiah's Mom was an impoverished single mom with no one to help her with Isaiah's daily care and no financial support. They were homeless.

Morgan, a child of 10, walked immediately over to Isaiah and talked to him for a considerable amount of time.

Isaiah looked at Morgan, grinning, eyes lit up, happy that someone was acknowledging him.

The next day we returned with another crate of shoes. Morgan said, "I'll be back in a minute, Mom. I'm going to visit Isaiah."

Unbeknownst to me, Morgan gave Isaiah the $ 7.00 his Grandma had given him for his birthday. The following day the Special Ed Teacher handed me a grateful thank you note from Isaiah's Mom. On the back of a torn, used envelope she wrote: "Thanks to your generous present, Morgan, I will be able to buy Isaiah a Christmas gift."

I had written the circumstances of The Washington Middle School homeless students to several Seattle philanthropists. Jack Benaroya called me upon receipt of his letter. He said he was sending me a check to pay for glasses and an eye exam one for one of the students who badly needed them, as he had worn glasses as a child.

The glasses and exam were a big hit and much appreciated by his family.

Washington Middle School also did not have any money to buy basketball uniforms for the boys' basketball program. The coach mentioned it to me, while I was watching a game the kids were playing in their street clothes. I had no money myself, barely scraping by, but I had an idea. I went to Sears on Lander Street and bought 16 jerseys on Leigh's Sears credit card! SCORE!!! The jerseys were only $ 3.99 each, but what a difference it made to that deserving basketball team.

Being Carded at GoodWill

During a recent Christmas Season, Paddy and I decided it would be nice to do something, however small, for some of the massive numbers of folks living under the freeway.

Warm winter gloves seemed doable.

I trekked to GoodWill, recalling they had large bags of fleece-lined gloves, 2 dozen pairs, for $ 65.00.

When it was my turn in line, I said, "The sign says you are offering 20% off today for seniors. May I take advantage of that?"

"NO!" the cashier snapped at me...

"Why would that be?"

"You have to be 52 years old," she replied, glaring at me suspiciously.

"I'm 77," I replied.

As she stared at me disdainfully, she growled, "Let me see your Drivers' License!" I complied.

Brow furrowed, the Cashier begrudgingly sold me the large package of fleece gloves for $ 52.00. Made my day! Carded at GoodWill.

On my way to my car in the cold rainy parking lot, I thought to myself: "Sheesh!....Did I just ask the GoodWill for a discount? How cheap could I be? With all the good they do for this community teaching literacy, job readiness and a hundred other things, I just asked for a DISCOUNT!!!!?" I was ashamed of myself.

Political, City, School and Charitable Campaigns:

Over the years I have worked on 22 political campaigns, in addition to arts, school and City campaigns; originally as a Republican, later as a Democrat; some as paid staff; some as a volunteer, including:

Paul Schell for Mayor - twice
Slade Gorton for Attorney General
Forward Thrust (Organized by Jim Ellis)
Save the Pike Place Market
Bruce Chapman for City Council
Teddy Kennedy for Senate (while living in Boston and Cambridge)
Joe Gandy for Governor
Dan Evans for Governor
Obama for President
PONCHO Auction (support for Seattle's arts community)
Channel 9 Fundraising Drive
Bertschi School Annual Auctions
St. Joseph School Auctions
O'dea School Annual Auctions
Treehouse for Kids Annual Galas and fund drives
Cornish College Annual Galas and fund drives
Seattle Art Museum Fundraising Campaigns and Galas
....in addition, **9 Non-Profit Boards**

Raising money for the non-profits remains a central commitment to myself, which is the primary responsibility of Board members.

I spent eight years on the Board of the Matt Talbot Homeless Shelter; helped found the Maude Fox Guild for the Childrens' Hospital; have spent the past 25 years on the Advisory Board and Board of Directors of TreeHouse for foster children, having launched it for Julia Calhoun. My previous deepest commitment was to Cornish College of the Arts, (of which I am an alum of the Fine Arts Department) where I donated 10 years as a Trustee, entailing over 7,500 volunteer hours, and sponsored 16 affluent people onto the Board when Cornish was on its knees financially. Cornish survived the crisis. It is now intrinsically a thriving element of Seattle's thriving arts community.

In 1985 A Seattle Art Museum Trustee put together a group of 80 women to raise money for the Seattle Art Museum. I was the 81st person to join. I also sponsored 22 more women. I also helped raise money for the Woodland Park Zoo and the Humane Society. I tried to be supportive of Morgan's schools by chairing procurement for the Morgan's private school auction, chairing the entertainment for the O'dea Scholarship Lunch, co-chairing the Artist in Residence program at St. Joseph School, chairing a fashion show benefit for Childrens' Hospital and several other community commitments. I chaired the Gala Opening of the Broadway Market, which was a split benefit between Cornish College of the Arts and the Seattle Art Museum. We made a lot of friends in the two years my enthusiastic committee of 144 people spent building this opening for both entities.

Seattle Infant Development Center

I am incredibly proud of spearheading the creation of the first Infant Day Care in downtown Seattle, or any other major American city in 1977. I had explored adopting a child myself, but discovered I could not manage to work and raise a child without accessible, affordable child care close to my office.

The City of Seattle was zoned to make such care impossible. I spent two years getting the city re-zoned, from King Street to Lenora, from First Avenue to 9th, with enormous help of then Congressman Norm Dicks, a college friend, who helped me achieve my 501c3. I put together a board, found space at the Plymouth Congregational Church on 6th Avenue and University Streets, and launched a center that celebrated its 42nd anniversary recently.

On 24-hours' notice, an NBC National News Cast and Crew flew up from Los Angeles to cover our big Opening Day a few days before we were ready. I " borrowed" babies for the cribs to "stand in" for those would-be initial infants.

My resourceful sister-in-law, Sally Davidson, loaned me her baby, Peter. She also corralled three of her friends to loan their infants, too.

After they deposited the little ones at 7:45 in the morning, I sent all the mothers across the street to the Olympic Hotel for breakfast. (In a time before cell phones,) after the news crew left, I dashed over to the Olympic to sound the "All Clear"....NBC did a fabulous story, while they had no idea the babies were fake tenants of my new Center. Whew!

After the NBC 6:00 Evening National News Feature on our "Seattle Infant Development Center" opening, I was able to consult by phone with New York, Dallas, Los Angeles, Chicago to help them get started, also, arranging "downtown daycare" for their working families in offices. No other such facility in the nation existed. I am proud of this accomplishment. Our first little childcare center in re-zoned Downtown Seattle has made an enormous impact across America for working parents; especially for nursing mothers.

While I was beginning my small business, after a divorce from Leigh, Julia Calhoun contacted me to create a visibility/launch for Treehouse for Kids— a non-profit, serving Foster Children in the King County area, and eventually throughout the state. She had a vision and some money, but relatively new to Seattle, had few contacts. I sent out a letter to 800 people I knew, in which I included, on a piece of flow-ered stationery, a small 2" x 4" dear letter from a 7-year-old girl – a thank you note for a used dress from the Treehouse "Wearhouse." Within 8 days, I received $48,000.00 in checks in the mail. Julia, Janis Avery and I were off and running with what has become, under Janis's incredible direction, a multi-million dollar operation, serving thousands of foster children state-wide each year.

Feature Film

In 1987, right after the Broadway Market Opening, a film enthusiast contacted me, asking me to finance a low-budget, two million dol-lar family film, "Journey to Spirit Island." A feature film had never been financed in Seattle, but my contact had a good script and cre-ative ideas in terms of director, cinematographer, actors, location, etc. The screenplay told the story of two Makah teenagers who lived near Cape Flattery, inviting urban cousins from Chicago for the summer -- a story of their adventures canoeing, camping out, and discovering a sacred Eagle's nest.

Of more interest to me than this specific movie per se was the fact that Seattle had no part in the lucrative film industry. All of the films being shot in the Northwest were being filmed in Vancouver and surroundings because they accommodated the film crews; in fact, courted them.

The Seattle City Officials made it very difficult to film here, which I didn't understand. The simplest thing, like closing off a block for an hour or two to shoot a scene was a nightmare of red tape. This made no sense to me, as the film crews rented hotel rooms, dined at restaurants, rented cars, bought gifts for their families, employed "extras", purchased equipment, hired consultants, makeup artists, logistics people and on and on. Their children did not use our free schools or cost Seattle one thin dime. Why wouldn't we want this lucrative business for Seattle's bottom line? As a Seattle tax payer, I was anxious to bring these luxury dollars to our city.

I set up the appointments to sell Limited Partnerships to finance the film. I was startled the first time I saw the film with my name, "Dee McQuesten-Davidson, Executive Producer" flashing across the big screen. We had wonderful local distribution at Alderwood, Kenny Alhadeff's Bay Theatre, Aurora Village Crossroads Parkway, Kent and Gateway. The film received great ratings as a 3 ½ Star family film up and down the West Coast, eventually available in VCR.. Ultimately it was sold to Disney for very little money. After spending hundreds of hours over two years to finance the film, I made $6,000 for selling two million dollars' worth of $25,000 part-nerships. Because of expenses, the film didn't make much money, but was still an exciting adventure for both myself and Morgan who flew to the San Juans with me via float plane when I had to attend the shoot. It was fascinating to learn how a film is built, edited and distributed.

It was pure joy working with the Makah Indian Nation, many of whom signed up as paid extras. We carried hundreds and hundreds of pounds of equipment through the forest to shoot scenes in Cape Flattery and Sucia Island. One of the very best aspects of the movie was Vilmos Sigmund who had previously earned an Oscar for his work on "Deer Hunter." He and Laszlo Pal, our Director, had escaped Hungary together when they were just 14 years old. Vilmos shot this movie as a favor to Las for $ 200,000, several million below his market rate. The way he captured the San Juan scenery and wild life was absolutely spectacular.

More recently I wrestled with an enduring local problem in Madison Park. For over 20 years I had written, called, texted, emailed the City of Seattle begging a clean-up of a dilapidated, unsightly series of shops in our neighborhood on Madison Street in Madison Park between 42nd and 41st on the north side of the street. 0 The building belonging to a well-known recluse and her mother for many, many decades, had fallen into dreadful dis-repair; the roof was caving, there were rats, the windows were boarded up and the environment and appearance seriously impacted the nearby shops and especially the nearby restaurant, now Madison Kitchen.

Having exhausted every avenue I could conjure up, I decided to visit our City Attorney, Pete Holmes. I took him statistics, photographs, measurements, etc. He immediately sent a team over to the owner's home in Montlake to do a Wellness Check. Though others had claimed nothing could be done, saying: "It was her property to do with as she pleased," Holmes used his office to force her to sell. Brian and Betsy Losh bought the building. George Meade is now renovating it into a lovely part of our little neighborhood village; a bookstore, antique shop, and an art studio. I am grateful to Pete Holmes for acting quickly and accurately. Our neighborhood is so much better off for his caring, concern and carefully aimed legal expertise.

Home Parish

As a 36-year member of a Catholic Lector Team, 18 years at St. Joseph Parish, I often read the first or second lesson or the

"Prayers of the Faithful" during Sunday Mass. One Sunday my friend Elizabeth Rudolf, who had spent many years working in and around theaters in New York, not a regular St. Joe's Parishioner, attended our parish for a special relative's Baptism. After Mass, she found me out on the front lawn and said, surprised: "Why dee, I didn't know you had a _speaking part_ in the Catholic Church!"

The Church Lady

In the mid 2000's, for about a year and a half, I served as a chaplain at Harborview Hospital, visiting and bringing Communion, saying Rosaries and other prayers in both English and Spanish, to and with the Catholic patients. -- the Tuesday Catholic "Chaplain."

My Supervising Catholic Chaplain, Theresa Litourneau, could not possibly have prepared me for what I would encounter. Fortunately, on my very first night on duty, Theresa wasby with me.

We walked into our first room where a beautiful young Latino man from Yakima, between 15 and 18, lay unconscious with at least 20 tubes connected to his head and chest. He had been brought by Harborview's Medi-Vac Trauma Team from Yakima. His Mother, also a strikingly beautiful woman, no more than 30, stood by his bed in silence, tears streaming down her face. Immediately I felt the pain she was experiencing, oh so deeply. Within 10 seconds tears streamed down my face, too. I asked her in Spanish if she would like me to say The Lord's Prayer with her. She nodded yes, so I took ahold of her hand and we wept through it together. I stood with my arm around her shoulder for another half an hour, then faded out of the room, not wanting to leave her, but with a list of 15 patients to visit.

One of the upsides of Harborview volunteer work is the doctors and nurses were wildly enthusiastic to see me coming down the hall. They always welcomed me gratefully, arms open, with a few special requests. It was gratifying to be an acknowledged member of a team I believed in.

The downside of Harborview work (or any hospital chaplaincy work) is you never know what has become of the patients you have counseled, prayed with – or just sat with. Since my shift was only Tuesdays, by the time I returned the following Tuesday, my patients had either recovered enough to go home, been sent to a rehab facility or died. To this day I wonder, with hope, whatever happened to that beautiful young man, riddled with bullet holes. And what about his Mother? Was she able to take him home? If he died, was she able to recover with some kind of peace – or did she have to live in anguish with a broken heart the rest of her life? Never having lost a grown child, the pain that parents feel at the loss of a child is far beyond my comprehension.

On another Tuesday, Theresa Litourneau and I spent some time with a badly beaten prostitute who had been left for dead on Airport Way. Thankfully, she had been found on the side of the road by a Good Samaritan and brought in to the Harborview Emergency Room. She was a tiny woman, about 5'2", maybe 80 pounds, approximately 50 years old. She told me how she desperately missed her 6 children, all of whom live in California. I promised her I would return to see how she was doing the next day. She told me she had no money to buy paper, envelopes and stamps to write to her children; all of whose addresses she knew by heart.

The following day I returned to her room with flowers from my garden, in a vase wrapped with pink ribbon, stamps, stationery and envelopes so she could write to her children. When I entered her room, about 4:00 in the afternoon, she screeched: "I have been waiting ALL day to go for a walk because I didn't want to miss the church lady!!!!" And then she began to cry, "No one has ever brought me flowers before." For several weeks thereafter Paddy smilingly referred to me as "the Church Lady."

Homeboy Locally

What I suspect will be my final foray into civic engagement is still on-going. It grows out of my childhood traumatic experience. I care so deeply about children, especially those who have been abused, those needing a chance as adults to live meaningful lives.

Some years ago, Paddy introduced me to Jesuit Father Greg Boyle from LA, when he visited Seattle. In 1987, Greg founded and still leads Homeboy Industries in Los Angeles, the largest operation in the world helping young people extricate themselves from gang activity and seeking work when they are released from incarceration. (Greg is the author of New York Times Best Seller *Tattoos on the Heart*, and more recently, *Barking to the Choir*)

Coincidently, a high school classmate, Susan Stephan Rosenberg, a volunteer Math and Language Arts Teacher at Homeboy for many years, had urged me to come look at this unique program helping gang-related and previously incarcerated young people.

Finally, 3 years ago, I visited. Immediately, I realized that something like this was needed in Seattle. I know something about abuse. I can, in a smaller but very real way, relate to these kids and what they endure at the hands of parents and others. It's astounding that many of them come out alive, much less have the drive to finish necessary education, and move on to jobs and/or even college.

The real beginning of this work came when I read with horror about Alajawan Brown in Seattle. He was 12. He was playing in a junior football league, dreaming of playing ball for Rainier Beach High School.

He asked his parents, Ayanna and Louis Brown for some cleats. His folks encouraged him to meander the neighborhood offering to mow friends' lawns, to earn the money for the cleats himself. He did!

On the afternoon of April 29, 2010, Alajawan stepped off a Metro Bus, his brand new cleats in hand, heading into a 7-Eleven on South 129th Street and Martin Luther King Way. A carload of Blood street gang members, stopped at a nearby red light, shot Alajawan in the back because he was wearing a blue and white jacket, the colors of a rival gang, the Crips.

As a mother, I followed this agonizing story in the Seattle Times for three years, wondering if there would be any consequences for the shooter, if he could even be identified. He was ultimately found, tried and sentenced to a 50-year prison term.

What a tragic waste of a bright, athletically talented, polite, kind 12-year-old! And 50 years in prison? What good does that do anyone? It chews up 50 years of someone's life to no avail, and costs our economy a ton of money per prisoner per day. The entire scenario felt disastrous and horrid for both Alajawan, his family and community, and the shooter, his family and community. Everyone loses.

Tragic for young people to drive around doing "revenge killings!" There must be some cure.

The April 16, 2017, Seattle Times photo of Alajawan's tearful parents, Mrs. Brown doubled over in tears, touched deeply into my soul, leaving a permanent lesion still today. I have been unable to walk away from that photo, nor erase it from my heart.

I decided to take my high school classmate's, Susan Stephan Rosenberg's, offer to visit Homeboy and see Greg Boyle once again. After that first visit, my mental machinery began to tick off all kinds of possibilities.

So, with the support, encouragement and wisdom of an amazing Advisory Board and Board of Directors, and especially Dan Quinn-Shea, CPA, sat with me for 11 ½ hours filling out the impenetrable 501c3 application to the IRS. With the help of our Congress Woman Pramila Jayapal's talented staff, we achieved our non-profit status.

I have traveled, now, to Homeboy LA eight times to work with Greg's crew, hoping to duplicate locally their spirit and approaches.

At the suggestion of Chuck Nordhoff, a steadfast friend who has stood by me throughout this project, I spent weeks, visiting in person, reading on-line and making phone calls, building a matrix of what agencies and groups provide services to this population in Seattle. Aided by a fellow St. Joe's Parishioner, Roger Rigor, a Math and Science teacher, I discovered a scarcely visible, but dynamic Academy in Columbia City.

Now our non-profit, *First Chance Industries*, provides a financial back up for this Academy covering some of their day-to-day emergencies; -- a cell phone for a student living in a dangerous situation; a $673 electric bill so students wouldn't be evicted within 6 hours; $10,000.00 over a two-year period, worth of Safeway Grocery Coupons so that families could eat during Thanksgiving and Christmas break; shoes that don't have holes in them for graduating seniors to wear with their caps and gowns. We were able to offer $100 for a student living in a dangerous situation, needing a cell phone; another needed a used baby stroller for her 2-week-old baby girl so she could set her down while she was in class — no family, no friends to help her, but she made it to class every morning, working hard to achieve her Diploma. That was March. She Graduated in June!

In 2020 the Academy, with their additional 11 mini-campuses, has 550 students, from 14 to 21: 112 are homeless; 42 have babies and toddlers of their own. The faculty and staff nurtures, educates, encourages, buoys and loves these kids into a new self-image, a high school diploma, a job and if appropriate, a pathway to college. I feel privileged to help.

I have learned a great deal over the past 4 years about young people inolved in gang activity. None are there because they want to be or because it is cool or because cousin Eddie belongs. None are running *to* gangs; they are running *from* abusive situations, looking for safety, having suffered every kind of abuse, imaginable and unimaginable. Usually, they discover gang life worse than what they were running from. Not all the Academy students are former gang members, but all have been through major traumas and toxic living environments that make school difficult.

According to Bobbe Bridge's (Founding President/CEO of the Seattle-based Center for Children & Youth Justice, Retired Justice on Washington State Supreme Court) staff, over 30,000 kids, across an 8-10 year period, are involved in gangs in the Seattle megalopolis area.

Over 70% of gang members are homeless. They are just like my Morgan or your kids, except that that no one ever wanted them or believed in them. A lot of their lives are thrown off track before they are born, to mothers who did not want to be pregnant. We call our organization "First Chance" because prior to walking through the doors of the Academy, they had no chance, no shot at life. All that changes when the faculty and staff begin to change their self-image, provide motivation and reduce their fears.

One story helps to typify what these kids have been through: little Tommy was playing on the floor with his brother and sister. Tommy was 5. Tommy's toy battery died. He ran to the bedroom to get a new battery and resumed play with his siblings. His father came home, not totally sober, yelling, "Where did you get that battery, Tommy?"

"In the top dresser drawer in the bedroom, Daddy, where you keep them."

"You are NEVER to steal anything out of my dresser, do you hear me?" "Yes, Daddy."

At which point Tommy's father took hold of Tommy's tiny little wrist and his elbow. He snapped his arm over his thigh and broke Tommy's arm in half! True story. Tommy was 5.

Such child abuse – and worse – is pervasive. It happens every-where, even in Seattle.

By the time Tommy was 8, he began looking around for a safe place to hide from his Dad. Eventually, he joined a gang, went to prison. Now he is part a program teaching self esteem. Without such a program, Tommy would have likely died in prison or on the street. Hallelujah!

It's appalling what toxic, angry parents, grandparents, siblings and neighbors do to children when fueled with alcohol and drugs and/or if they are mentally ill.

This gifted Academy faculty meets the students where they are and often, literally, loves and encourages them back to life, helping discover their own gifts and talents, and grow into the person they were meant to be. At the Academy, in spite of what these students have been through, they persevere a high school diploma, jobs and some a college degree. The Academy, with its healing heart, graduated 140 students in June of 2019, 30 of whom were in King County Jail or the Juvenile Detention Center, where there are also Academy faculties.

Every Friday morning the Academy has "Orientation" from 9 – 11. They take aspiring students from 14 to 21. Anyone who walks in the door. Teens hear about this program on the street, sometimes from other schools, sometimes from their Probation Officers or Juvenile Court.

For the teens who see something they like in the Friday morning orientation, the following 5 schooldays are spent at the Academy in full-blown academic and psychological testing. At the end of that 5-day period, the potential student meets with family, if they have any, some faculty and the Academy School Principal and Vice Principal to determine which of the 12 small campuses would serve each individual student best.

Campuses are strategically located city-wide, some for specific kinds of students. For instance, the Recovery School campus serves specifically kids who are struggling really hard to get off alcohol and drugs. There are a couple of campuses in West Seattle; one for girls only. Another campus is housed in a donated airplane wing where students learn wood working, welding, etc., along with their academics. Two campuses are for incarcerated youths -- the Juvenile Justice Center and the King County Jail. All students have to pass the same Math, Science, English tests etc., as mainstream Washington State high school students to receive diplomas.

Father Greg used to say "Nothing stops a bullet like a job." Now he says "Nothing stops a bullet like a healing heart."

From my own abusive upbringing, I have some deep understanding of trauma, of why these kids can't focus in Seattle's mainstream public high schools. I know what that feels like. I know how they often feel -- a bother and an *inconvenience* to their birth parents and/or various, multiple temporary living situations. I salute these young people who work their way into a different kind of life, driven by determination and life-changing goals taught at the Academy, in Father Greg's Homeboy Industries in L.A., and at the Nativity School in Seattle's Central District.

While I have done no actual "fundraising" for First Chance, it has been surprisingly gratifying to see how many people, just knowing a little about the school, and even hearing about it in casual conversations, by word of mouth, have given me financial help for the students; funds to back them up, primarily for emergencies and Safeway Grocery Coupons.

Ten, twenty and thirty years from today the world (and our city) will be a better place because we loved these kids. To me, obviously, these children and teens are not "somebody else's" responsibility because, most of the time, the "somebody else" who birthed them, doesn't give a rip about them. *THEY ARE INCONVENIENT!* I don't believe in throwing teens and children away.

Sometimes it only takes one person to help get a life on track. Oh, how I wish each of these kids had a loving Gran. How different their life would be. But I do see, however, many Grans at the Academy, around 76 of them. I watch the kids connect with them. I see the alums walking down the hallways to visit some of their favorite teachers. Every time I stop by school, usually 2 or 3 times a week, some faculty member introduces me to an alum or two who popped by to check in. Their connection is for life; not just for a few short years. They know how much they are valued by each and every faculty and staff member. The Academy is their forever family.

Presently First Chance is reaching down to the next age group — middle school at the Nativity School on Massachusetts Street. All students in this program are on scholarship, some traveling round-trip up to four hours a day to attend! While the Society of Jesus provides general endorsement and oversees the high quality STEM education (Science, Technology, Engineering and Mathematics), money is less than thin; we can help.

I could (and hope to) work this project helping to lift up young people until my dying breath . At that point, whenever that day comes, I will still be grateful for having had the opportunity.

Joel Pritchard, U.S. HUD Director having a Pike
Place Market Tour with dee McQuesten

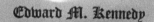

Edward M. Kennedy

July 8, 2008

Ms. Dee McQuesten
2460 Canterbury Ln. E.
Apt. 1-A
Seattle, WA 98112

Dear Ms. McQuesten:

Thank you so much for your prayers and good wishes. They mean so much to both of us as we face this new and unexpected health challenge.

We are deeply grateful for your thoughtfulness.

Sincerely,

Ted and Vicki Kennedy

Ted and Vicki Kennedy

Letter from Ted and Vicki Kennedy when his brain tumor was first diagnosed...2008

*Madison Park newspaper founded, published, edited and delivered
by dee McQuesten-Davidson, beginning December 12, 1980.*

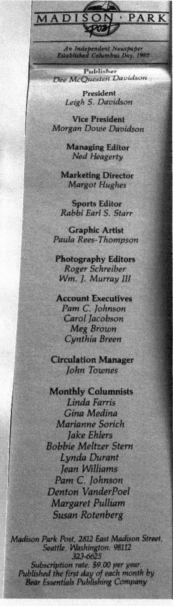

MADISON · PARK

An Independent Newspaper
Established Columbus Day, 1980

Publisher
Dee McQuesten Davidson

President
Leigh S. Davidson

Vice President
Morgan Dowe Davidson

Managing Editor
Ned Heagerty

Marketing Director
Margot Hughes

Sports Editor
Rabbi Earl S. Starr

Graphic Artist
Paula Rees-Thompson

Photography Editors
Roger Schreiber
Wm. J. Murray III

Account Executives
Pam C. Johnson
Carol Jacobson
Meg Brown
Cynthia Breen

Circulation Manager
John Townes

Monthly Columnists
Linda Farris
Gina Medina
Marianne Sorich
Jake Ehlers
Bobbie Meltzer Stern
Lynda Durant
Jean Williams
Pam C. Johnson
Denton VanderPoel
Margaret Pulliam
Susan Rotenberg

Madison Park Post, 2812 East Madison Street,
Seattle, Washington, 98112
323-6625
Subscription rate: $9.00 per year.
Published the first day of each month by
Bear Essentials Publishing Company

Masthead for Madison Park Post...note Vice President:
Morgan Dowe Davidson...January, 1982

dee McQuesten serving Foster Families in Treehouse "Wearhouse"...2018

As Executive Producer of "Journey to Spirit Island", I set up appointments to fund a family film we shot in the San Juan Islands....my underlying purpose was to get a film industry started in Seattle, as it was all going to Vancouver, B.C....Our rating was 3 ½ stars, which was considered high, especially for a family film.

Original staff of the Madison Park Post....1983

Micah at Academy Graduation...2019

Micah's Hands composing on a donated Academy Piano...Micah played a piece he composed during the Graduation Ceremony...2019

Academy Graduation in Seattle's High School Memorial Stadium…..Tears and cheers all around for how hard these kids have worked against **unimaginable** *odds to achieve their High School Diplomas…June, 2019*

Pat Carroll, Jesuit Father Greg Boyle and a beloved
Homeboy…Los Angeles ….2020

Victor Verdugo and dee McQuesten in Father Boyle's office…January, 2020

Melissa Rysemus, dee McQuesten, Jesuit Father Greg Boyle,
Kaaren Andrews, Randy Novak; all First Chance Board Members...
dinner in a Los Anglese Restaurant...October, 2019

dee McQuesten at Homeboy Industries
compound with Recycle Truck...2018

Framed quilt in Homeboy Industries Embroidery and Tee-Shirt Printing Shop...Los Angeles...2019

dee McQuesten with L.A.'s Finest...2018

*Kaaren Andrews speaking at the First Chance Website Launch
Party at Sarah Alexandra's Shoppe on Madison Street...
background: Emery Walters and Pam Schell...2019*

First Chance Website Launch Party...Winnie Sperry, Pam Schell,
Bob Davidson, Tienny Milnor, John Hayes, Melissa Rysemus...2019

*Special cake from Chuck Nordhoff and Maribeth O'Connor
when they hosted a First Chance Board dinner...2018*

Dear thank you note from an Academy student who was happy to have help with day care for her toddler...2019

*Madison Park store front after Pete Holmes, Seattle City
Attorney, responded to dee's plea to clean up the boarded
building on Madison Street between 41st and 42nd Avenue East;
now beautifully renovated by George Mead; later purchased
by Brian and Betsy Losh, Ewing & Clark... 2020*

dee McQuesten, Tom Skerritt, Kayla Skinner...Opening Night
Premier Gala for "A River Runs Through It"...1992

*Home of Homeboy Industries Los Angeles...three stories include
bakery, gift shop, café, tattoo removal, classrooms and offices*

dee McQuesten with Jesuit Father Greg Boyle in his office...2017

Los Angeles Mayor's Office houses a modest Homeboy Cafe...2018

CHAPTER ELEVEN

Impoverished Freedom

After I separated from Leigh, Morgan and I picked out an apartment in Madison Park with two small bedrooms. Too soon I became aware that women over 50 were not easily employable in Seattle in 1993. Despite my education and quite varied work experiences, my age made health insurance prohibitive to employers. I experienced a much broader Ageism than expected. I was 52.

Soon into my single mom voyage, I applied for a job seen in the newspaper at an employment agency in downtown Seattle. The woman who interviewed me was wildly enthusiastic. She said I was perfect for a receptionist position at a downtown law firm and set up an appointment.

I arrived the next morning in my black suit and heels to be escorted to the firm for an interview. A man in the employment office appeared down the hallway, saying, "No way! You are totally inappropriate for this job. They want someone young, energetic and attractive. You would never do and you are too old!" I was 52.

Though insulted and hurt at the time, if I had taken the position, I may have never founded my own company; in retrospect, he probably did me a painful favor!

My primary reason for separating from Leigh was to extricate my child from an overwhelmingly unhealthy alcohol environment. Leigh was a good money manager. I had always given him my paychecks, which he banked in a joint account. After he said, "*But who's going to do the laundry?*" he quickly closed the account with all of my paychecks therein. I left a marriage, again, without a penny. There was just enough money from Gran's estate to pay for four years of Morgan's O'Dea tuition through his high school and his first year of college. I wouldn't spend a cent of that money. It was too important for my child's education.

Leigh and I had joint custody. I drove Morgan to school, picked him up after. I stayed as close by as I could, vigilant of his ongoing activities and participating in his school life. There were some very thin financial times.

Morgan's attendance at O'Dea was one of many, many major disagreements Leigh and I had. Morgan had his heart set on O'dea. I felt he was old enough to participate in the choice of his 4-year high school. Leigh insisted Morgan should attend Roosevelt or Garfield. Morgan was right. He made many life-long friends, played football for 4 years, and remains active there, after all these years since graduation in 2000, as a vital member of their football coaching squad.

My friends buoyed my spirits by encouraging me during the time after I left Morgan's dad. I was living in a basement apartment with no heat. At Christmas time, Mardy and Bob Sander gave me a large plug-in heater that heated the whole apartment. Mardy saw that I was wasting away, down to 105 pounds and said, "You should come here for dinner – every night!" I didn't do that, even one night, but having been given such a magnanimous invitation, my spirits were boosted.

I could not find a full-time job. The only thing I had was good credit. I took out a $10,000.00 loan for rent, groceries, a used car and car insurance, etc., which didn't last long. I baby sat and found other part-time work at Barnes and Noble cashiering evenings and weekends and some temporary work through agencies. With great satisfaction, if very little money, I worked as a Litigation Paralegal on Chris Gregoire's suit of the Tobacco industry when she was Attorney General of Washington state. Watching her was amazing. The opposition rolled in dolly after dolly after dolly of 4-drawer file cabinets. Gregoire arrived with a single briefcase; all needed information in her head. She proceeded to win.

Every time.

I also served as a substitute teacher or "para professional" in Special Ed in Seattle Public Schools. Eventually I found another part-time job for King County Public Defense interviewing inmates (clients) at the King County Jail, Region Justice Center, Municipal Court and the Juvenile Justice Center on behalf of King County Public Defense to determine who needed pro-bono legal assistance.

Not all was dour, while scrambling around trying to eek out a Living. One afternoon, while interviewing inmates at the King County Jail on James Street, I interviewed a drug dealer/pimp who asked if I would like to join his stable of "escorts." He assured me I would make a lot more money than whatever King County was paying me! Apparently in this line of work, age was not a limiting factor! Despite my financial predicament, I declined the offer.

When my friend, the wonderful Paul Schell was elected Seattle Mayor, he helped me get a job with the Mayor's Senior Citizen Office in Public Relations.

I did a myriad of other jobs while beginning my framing business on nights and weekends. Knowing my employment frustrations, my friends, Mary Snyder, Burnley Snyder and Debbie Blethen began encouraging me to take a hobby I was fairly good at, and start my own picture framing business. I always managed to feed Morgan decent meals, but there were very little left over funds. I lived for 3 ½ years on one bowl of Grapenut Flakes and orange juice four times a day. No protein, except on the rare dinner date. During that period of time I did not catch one cold or the flu. No cough, no sore throats, nothing. I'm pretty sure there was an Angel standing on my shoulder shooing all the bugs and germs away. Remind me to thank her!

A handful of my friends loaned me money to help pay rent and buy groceries periodically, all of whom I reimbursed, some with interest. The largest loan of $5,250 was harder to repay. I sold my treasured baby grand piano to cover that loan.

One Thanksgiving weekend, having managed to *scrape* together enough money to buy 800 Kinko's three cent copies, 800 envelopes and 800 stamps, I mailed out letters to announce I was starting a framing business. I offered complimentary pick-up and delivery service.

Within three days of mailing out my 800 letters, while I was hanging on for dear life, getting thinner and thinner, near malnutrition at 105 pounds, Alice Canlis phoned, saying: "dee, we have just completed a multi-million-dollar renovation of our Canlis Restaurant. I could use some help." She ordered 92 new frames! HOORAY! I marched directly to Bert's, our local market, bought a pound of hamburger, made paddies and ate them all the same night! The first time I had been able to buy protein for myself in 3 ½ years.

Alice Canlis, in turn, referred me to a couple of people, who told others and my still largely word-of-mouth business, now

McQuesten Framing and Fine Arts Services, was on its way, now almost 30 years old and modestly successful. Along the way, I have expanded to art restoration, art and mirror installation, and art shipping. I have met a huge variety of people over the nearly 30 years of service – some nice, some interesting, some not so nice, some amazing.

One client who is permanently lodged in heart is a young mother who came to my studio a year ago, asking if I could frame approximately 20 pieces of her little boy's art. Having looked it over, I said, "This is very good art for a little boy. How old is your son"? She replied: "He was 8. He died 6 weeks ago – of cancer." I felt like I had been hit by a freight train! Soooo hard to imagine how this young mother must have been feeling.

For a single underemployed mid-age woman, transportation was an issue. I initially purchased a Volvo Station Wagon from Sound Ford. Within a year it needed engine work I could ill afford. I returned to Sound Ford and asked if there was possibly a less expensive car I could trade for the wagon. They quickly traded me an old small 2-door Subaru stick shift. 24 hours later the engine died while I was driving up Roy Street on the West Side of Capitol Hill. A mechanic helped me get started. Morgan helped me drive it back to Sound Ford on Rainier Avenue in Renton. I handed them the keys, explaining I was canceling my brand new contract; the car was a total lemon. I was not going to pay to fix it. Two men at the front desk insisted: "You didn't buy that piece of S—t here!" I assured them I did indeed. Morgan and I drove away.

Two days later a Special Delivery Courier brought an invoice to my door for $125.00 for towing my car, left by Sound Ford at a Wendy's directly across the street from the car dealership on Rainier Avenue! I contacted a friend, Art Harrigan, smartest litigator in Seattle, and said "What do I do? These people play dirty. And I have very little money." Art referred me to one of his partners, Matthew, who did some Pro Bono legal work each month. After much legal wrangling and maneuvering on Matt's part, Sound Ford canceled my Subaru contract and took care of the towing bill.

My Other Boys

I cannot tell the story of my life and omit one – really two- enormous delights for the last eleven years. My niece, Cathy, had twins in 2008. She was alone and working full time, with a daytime nanny. She could not get out to buy diapers, a cup of coffee, and, like any mom, she needed a break!

Her step-mother, Fran Davidson, suggested that Cathy needed help. Since Paddy and I rarely went out at night, maybe it would be nice to give Cathy a hand. So it began – one of the most wonderful sagas of my life – every Friday night, some Tuesdays and sometimes Sundays with Tanner and Chase Davidson, from infancy on. Two more dear little boys there never were, energetic, polite, bright and eager to please.

One night Tanner did not like the dinner I cooked for him. He was 2. He yelled at me. I said, "Tanner, when you yell at me, it hurts my feelers." At which point, Chase said, "Yeah, Tanner, and when you yell at deedee, it hurts MY feelers, too!"

Pure joy, these two little boys. At first they were skeptical of me; then I began getting occasional phone calls from them on the nights I was not with them. Cathy said they just needed to visit a minute. They needed a deedee hit!

When they were tiny, I carried them up the stairway to the nursery at bath and bedtime one at a time. Eventually, when they were older, they began to climb the stairs themselves with me close behind them. One night they chatted and chatted and chatted after I put them in their cribs. There was no way I could get to them to consider sleeping. We had a tradition that each boy could choose three books that I would read to them and the 7th book was my choice. Always "Good Night, Good Night Construction Site." I loved that book, as did the boys.

During the period when Cathy was potty training the boys, I was leaving the playroom for a minute because I had to run to the potty myself. Chasey jumped up, saying "I'll help you, deedee!" His Mommy had been helping him, so he knew how to do it!

Eventually they became young men and began to have opinions and worries. One Saturday I arrived to drive them to Montlake soccer practice when Cathy was busy. Tanner began to cry: "You can't take us, deedee, because you don't know the way?" Absolutely terrified that he would miss practice, we somehow fumbled and bumbled our way to the Montlake Fieldhouse where I had been several hundred times!

Wonderful Stories Abound!

One night, when Tanner was 3, he went into TOTAL meltdown when the top of his banana broke off – he really hates anything to break. We were all sitting at the kitchen table after dinner. Chase and I tried and tried to talk him down. Finally, when I distracted him with a graham cracker, he stopped crying, and Chasey suggested: "Tanner, use your shirt to wipe the tears off your face." Tanner complied immediately; everyone seemed happy and ready to move on.

Something terribly funny or warmly delightful happened almost every evening or afternoon I spent with the boys. Chasey decided he was hungry about half way through his cousin Grey Davidson's final U Prep basketball game. I had a sack of emergency snack food. I offered Chasey a banana, which he took, sitting behind me on Uncle Bobby's lap. I turned around to watch the game. Minutes later, I felt a tap-tap-tap on my left shoulder. I turned around and saw Chasey's bewildered little pink face. He said "deedee, open it!", handing the banana back to me.

After we had dinner one summer night, we went to the Madison Park Playground. The slide was very large. I said it looked like fun; could I slide down, too? In unison, they both insisted: "NO! You have to be a KID," Tanner adding: "You're too old and you'll get hurt!"

Once Cathy and I took separate boys on Saturday on a play date. I took Chasey to the Big Wheel on the waterfront. Chasey said, just before we boarded: "deedee, if I get scared, can I sit on your lap?" I said "Okay, but if I get scared first, can I sit on yours?"

One Friday Tanner asked me to cut an orange in squares for him, so, I sliced it in circles; then cup each circle in small ½" squares. Tanner was absolutely delighted; you would have thought I just built the Taj Mahal.

I called the boys one evening to check in and say hello because they LOVE getting phone calls and, having a bad sinus infection, I didn't want them to think I had forgotten them. Chase got right on the phone with great enthusiasm and said "deedee, we can't come over right now because we are eating French fries!"

One night after bubble baths and 7 story books I could not get the boys to stop chattering and sleep — lot of excuses: "deedee, I need a drink of water"... on and on. By pure happenstance, Morgan popped in. I told him I was worried they would feel awful the next day if they didn't go to sleep. Morgan marched upstairs into the nursery. In his most authoritative O'Dea Football Coaching voice: "Alright, boys, the next one who says one single word sleeps in the garage tonight!" It was January; never another peep. The house was suddenly very still.

My life has been filled for 10 years with the joys of experiencing these two dear little fellows and their new 11-year-old brother, Gavin, and 13-year-old sister, Maddy – lots of homework, baseball, basketball, T-ball, Lacrosse, jog-a-thons, Halloweens, Christmases, Easters and soccer games. No greater thrill have I than to watch these four young athletes hone their skills and grow now, nearly into middle school.

Recently I was parking the car at Bert's Grocery here in the neighborhood. When I emerged from the car, there was Tanner coming down the sidewalk on his bicycle; seeing me, he stopped instantly and visited for an extended time. What 11-year-old boy visits with a boring grown-up!? Amazing!!!

Chase and Tanner liked to read Morgan's
childhood books at bedtime....2013

Paddy reading to Tanner and Chase Davidson during a sleepover...2015

Tanner and Chase liked a bubble bath before bedtime stories

*Paddy is the all-time great bedtime story book
reader....during a 2016 sleepover*

*Morgan napping after a romp with Tanner, left
and Chase, right; all sound asleep...2014*

Chase and Tanner at Madison Park Pre-School...2013

Cathy Davidson, Tanner Davidson, Chase Davidson, Gavin Nolz, Maddy Nolz, Pat Carroll Presiding, Jon Nolz Photo by Debra Drake 2015

Wedding Day: Jon Nolz, Cathy Davidson, Gavin Nolz,
Pat Carroll presiding, Maddy Nolz...August, 2015

Tanner and Chase Davidson playing soccer in dee's
back yard at Edgewater after a sleepover and
alphabet pancakes, Paddy's specialty…2015

Jon Nolz, very best Dad and Coach in the world...2016

Tanner Davidson gearing up for a game of LaCrosse...2020

*Chase and Tanner about to launch two kayaks
on Lake Washington...2019*

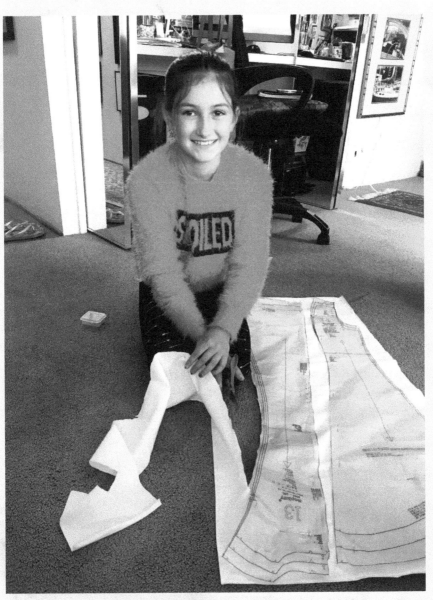

deedee and Maddy building a new dress...2018

*Maddy's new dress finished...a good
beginning sewing adventure...2017*

CHAPTER TWELVE

The Rest of the Story

What Ever Happened to?..........

Gran McQuesten, my adoptive nurturing Mother (previously my maternal Grandmother), Maybelle LaPlante McQuesten, born May 14, 1893, died in Yakima, Washington, December 13, 1980, at 88, of Liver Cancer, the Sunday before my son, Morgan Dowe Davidson, was born. A Registered Nurse during the Spanish Flu, at Tacoma General Hospital, she and one other nurse were the 2 sole survivors. All of the patients, doctors, nurses and staff died. When she married September 1, 1919, she resigned from the hospital, as it was not proper for married women in those days to work outside the home; especially not a Senator's wife.

George Dowe McQuesten, my adoptive and nurturing Father, born in Litchfield, New on March 20, 1871, died in Sunnyside, Washington, December 11, 1965, of Prostate Cancer, having recently retired from law and residential housing development. My sister/Aunt, Emily, having conquered both Breast Cancer and Multiple Sclerosis years before, died in 1985 of Multiple Myeloma in Grandview, Washington, while happily married to her second husband, George Fitzpatrick. An accomplished woman, she worked for President John F. Kennedy in 1961 and 1962.

My brother/Uncle Joey, a widower, a retired CPA and chain smoker, died in Selah, Washington, in 2007 of Emphysema, happily re-married.

My Birth father, Alfred William Hawkins, a Railroad Fireman for the Burlington Northern, an alcoholic, re-married, died at age 45 of a heart attack in 1966 in Eastern Washington.

My Birth mother, Rosemary McQuesten, an alcoholic, drug addict and chain smoker, died at age 72 alone in Mesa, Arizona, having retired from Stanford University Hospital as a Secretary.

Besieged with severe diabetes and unable to feel his feet, Terry accidentally tripped over his small white Scotty Dog in his kitchen and tumbled down his cellar steps.

I have been told he fractured his skull and broke many bones, resulting in a long-term stay at Harborview Hospital. During his rehabilitation period at Skyline, he fell hopelessly in love with his Caretaker. He divorced his second wife and married his Caretaker, while confined to a wheelchair. He died shortly thereafter at age 75. I went to visit him for an hour a couple of months before he died. We married too young. We were children at age 20. Gran wept and begged me to wait until I finished college. She was right.

Leigh Shipman Davidson, some years after our divorce, contracted MS, which impacted him severely. He subsequently remarried. Unfortunately, however, the carbonated pop he consumed daily with his "adult beverage" dissolved his heart muscle, confining him, also, to a wheelchair, resulting in his tragic early death at 72 of Congestive Heart Failure. Paddy and I went to visit Leigh at Skyline just prior to his death, but he was out of the building at a medical evaluation. Tragically, Leigh Graduated and moved on to Heaven only a couple of days after that.

5:30 Daily Mass and a Miracle at St. James

Some six years after Leigh and I parted, while I was again cobbling five part-time jobs together: cashiering at the University Village Barnes & Noble; teaching English in Seattle Community College's ESL Program; interviewing inmates ("clients") at the King County Jail, Courthouse and the Regional Justice Center in Kent for King County Public Defenders, to determine who needed Pro Bono Legal Services, subbing in the Seattle Public School System; and making picture frames at home in my Edgewater Apartment. I met again a Jesuit Priest on Medical Leave, Pat Carroll, at the St. James evening weekday Mass. Pat had been a Pastor at St. Joseph's parish On Capitol Hill, some 23 years before where I met him only once, but significantly, for about 5 minutes, asking him for help for a dying friend of Pam Schell's and mine, Jody Sylvester, who was one of his Parishioners.

During Paul Schell's first campaign for Mayor in 1977, I managed his campaign office – not the campaign, but the volunteer squadron. A lovely young mother, Jody Sylvester, and her 10-year-old son, Michael, came to the office several nights a week, two of about 350 volunteers, to help me stuff envelopes and put out mailings. Jody always wore a maternity smock. We all assumed she was expecting another baby. She was a 6:25 a.m. Daily Communicant at St Joseph Parish before she readied Michael for school. One morning, after the campaign was long over, Paul's wife, Pam Schell, phoned to say we had been terribly wrong. Jody was not expecting; she had an inoperable stomach tumor, now so large she could no longer drive her car, much less get to Morning Mass. Pammie said, "You are Catholic. Can't you **DO** something?"

I did not know anyone at St. Joseph's Church, but I promised I would hop in my car on my lunch hour and see what I could do. At noon, I burst through the big brass double doors on the front of St. Joe's almost running into an also, rushing tall, slim curly-headed man, dressed in clerics with the traditional white stiff collar. I said, wisely; "You look like you work here; I need some help for my friend." The priest was Pat Carroll. In just a few moments, I had explained my mission. He agreed to go that day to visit Jody. "'Father Carroll" took Communion to Jody at home that afternoon and almost every day thereafter until she died 6 months later, when he presided at her funeral, by then a dear friend. Most heartbreaking in this story, for me, was little Michael, who adored his mother. The afternoon Jody died, Michael walked into the Madison Park Floral Shop and asked my friend, Steve Gleuck, if he would help him choose some flowers for his mother's funeral. That was in 1978.

Twenty-three years later, serendipitously, Father Carroll, now on a leave-of absence from the Jesuits, suffering from heart ailments, began to regularly attend the St. James Cathedral 5:30 p.m. Mass. With only about 30 or so people in attendance, everyone soon becomes a familiar face. I saw a distinctly Irish mug and knew I recognized him from *somewhere*.

One evening, as we walked out at the same time I asked him, "Aren't you Father Carroll?" He said yes, he used to be; now he was just Pat Carroll, working for the Sisters of Providence, on Medical Leave from the Jesuits. I exclaimed what wonderful care he had given our cherished Jody Sylvester before she died. Pat admitted, "I don't recognize you, but I remember our conversation." He explained his present situation and why, now living just two blocks away, he was a regular at that evening Mass. (To this day, Father Mike Ryan, Pastor of St. James Cathedral, claims we owe him a "Finders' Fee", as we connected at a St. James Mass!) I'll bake him some cookies!

Pat also lamented that it was difficult living alone in an apartment, especially eating dinner by himself. Though he had Jesuit colleagues living in near-by Arrupe House at Seattle University, he was trying to make some more friends. He had entered the Jesuits just after his 18th birthday; he had lived in community all these years. He asked, quite carefully, if I would you like to come for a Scotch or a tea or whatever I drank, after Mass some evening? He told me of his apartment at the Tate Mason, a low income building, just a block away. He had furnished his first-ever apartment by Share House, Goodwill and the Salvation Army. He'd been given some dishes, glasses and silverware, and was pretty much all set.)

Of course I would, I replied. What fun! I would love that! What a cool single pal to have, so highly educated, loving coffee and conversation. I should be lucky to have this man for a pal. Father Joe Kramis had been a good pal. Mary Kay Dyckman, Libby Moscardini and I had socialized with Joe for years until he moved to St. Therese in Federal Way, sooooo far away. Also, I had known Father Bob Camuso before he became a priest in his forties, and we sometimes had dinner or went to a movie. I suspected that with Pat, I just struck pay dirt. I told him to let me know when it worked for him. Though I was balancing a lot of different shifts between Barnes & Noble, substituting for the School District, doing interviews at the King County Jail and making picture frames at night, I definitely would find time.

Days later, one Wednesday as we left evening Mass, Pat caught up to me saying: "How 'bout tonight? Can you come by?" I had planned to finish a couple of picture frames but I could put them off til Thursday. "Let's do it. I'd love to see your place!"

I knew Pat had spent a year in Africa, many years at an inner-city parish in Tacoma, and at St. Aloysius on the Gonzaga University Campus, etc. It would be fascinating to hear about his journeys. This should be good, right? I had never seen a bachelor pad that wasn't a total mess, however. I was braced. Au contrere! Pat's tiny home was immaculate. The dishes were all put away in his miniscule kitchen. His small living room and bedroom were tidy. The bed was made. All the clothes were hung up. The towels were folded. I had walked into a miracle! The thrift shop furniture was a bit rumpled, but he had hung a clean throw over a comfy overstuffed chair. Everything looked fine and carefully arranged in front of the television.

Pat had no tea, but I carried emergency teabags in my purse, so I was prepared. We talked for a couple of hours, discovering multiple mutual acquaintances and interests in golf, tennis, literature, the-ater, on and on. After two hours, Pat said, "I have to cook dinner for myself. Won't you stay so we can continue our conversation?" We had the worst meal I had ever been invited to! He pulled out of the freezer a can of peas and put them in a dry pan. Then added a box of whole wheat noodles. Next, a can of tuna squeezed dry. He mixed it all together and served me a GINORMOUS mound! He said: "I want you to have enough to eat, as I know you work very hard." To which, after a single bite, I replied, "You know, I think I'll take you up on that glass of red wine." One bite of dry noodles, one gulp of wine; one bite of noodles; one gulp of wine 'til I had gone through two glasses!

Soon, it was time to leave. As we stood at his front door, I thought "This dear man needs a good home-cooked meal," and said, "On Sundays Morgan and I always have a special dinner. Would you like to join us sometime?" He asked where I lived. When I told him Madison Park, in the Edgewater apartments, he said, "No thanks. I wouldn't be interested." Had I missed something here? Didn't we have such a good conversation that he had asked me to stay a little longer?

I asked, "Why not?" "It's too far away." "Would you like my son to pick you up? Do you not have a car? Morgan is a junior at O'Dea; He'd be glad to pick you up — it's only about 5 minutes down the hill."

Still, he was not interested. Something was missing; Oh well. Back to my real life. It had been a delightful evening. I know now Pat was unsure of his future, uneasy feeling his way and, however much he enjoyed the evening, wary of entanglement.

About three weeks later, I saw Pat after a Saturday Morning Mass at the Cathedral. He was surrounded by at least 5 fawning single women. I waved at him, but he didn't see me - or perhaps just didn't acknowledge me. Oh well. He apparently wasn't interested in getting together again.

Two weeks later, one Sunday night at 8:00, Pat called just at the end of dinner. He said he had just finished a book he thought I'd like and he'd bring it to the evening Mass on Monday. I told him that Morgan and I had just finished dinner and hadn't cut the pie yet. Why didn't he come down the hill and join us for dessert? Pat said, "Oh no. I can't do that. It's too late at night."

"I thought you said Mondays were your days off. It's only 8 o'clock." "They are, but I never go out this late at night."

"You know, I think there's a bottle of scotch in the cabinet over the stove." "What's your address?" Pat arrived 10 minutes later.

We talked another couple of hours in front of a roaring fireplace. Pat read aloud -- Emily Dickinson and other poetry from Gran's book collection.

He called two days later and invited me back to his home for dinner. He said he'd rather have dinner at his house than mine. Okay. No explanation. Fine. Whatever. I enjoyed his dinner table about three times a week for the next several weeks. One evening he said, "You know, I think I'm going to have to get married." I replied, "I didn't think Priests could marry." He said, "Actually, I have a new life now, working for the Sisters of Providence, so it's my decision." "Terrific", I replied, "I can introduce you to half a dozen women friends who are pediatricians, lawyers, bankers; highly intelligent professional women you might enjoy." No response. We continued our dinner thing for a couple more months and one sunny Saturday I convinced him I knew how to cook and would he like to come by for Saturday supper?

I put a lot of effort into cooking a cold veal dish, cold salad and cold dessert. It was a glorious early spring warm 80 degree day. My whole west dining room wall was glass; it was scorching. Pat sat down, took one bite and said, "To me, dinner is a hot meal." I then realized Jesuits, or at least, Pat, had been so sheltered, free of female companionship, that his conversation was totally unfiltered. Refreshing, but often startling!

We continued dinner at Pat's apartment several times a week for another couple of months until one night he said, again, "You know, I think I'm going to have to get married." Again, I responded I told you I would be delighted to introduce you some terrific women. Pat surprised me with: "Actually, I was thinking of marrying **you!**"

Me? Really? Whew! Can we talk about this, because I don't really intend to marry again.

Pat's brother and sister-in-law were having a hard time accepting his decision to leave the priesthood and the Jesuits. At Thanksgiving his brother John told him that if he felt the need to bring me with him to Thanksgiving Dinner, it would be better that he not come at all. We were somewhat taken back, but Pat said, "Why don't you cook a turkey and you, Morgan and I will celebrate at your place in front of a nice fire. Which we did. I began at 4:30 that morning, making stuffing and yams, putting a large turkey in the oven and basting it, baking pies, on and on. It was a fun evening and Pat's comfort with teenagers shone through. Morgan was a lounger in those days, sprawled across the whole sofa so no one else could sit. With a smirk, Pat asked him "Is there anything else I can do for you or get for you to make you more comfortable?" The whole day was a treat!

The Wedding: Storm Drains, Judge Raines and Braziers

A year later, after Pat had applied to Rome for permission to marry but had not yet received any word, we were married in the little Chapel at Seattle Prep by a Catholic Judge friend, from my Court House work, Albert Raines. Pat's Jesuit cousin, Paul Fitterer, President of Seattle Prep at the time, offered Mass for family and close friends after the Civil Ceremony. Pat and I served Communion. Father John Coleman came up from Loyola Marymount University in Los Angeles to do the Homily. Morgan began the ceremony by lighting the wedding candle. Pammie Schell stood up with me and Paul Schell, now Seattle Mayor, read the Gospel. I dropped Pat's wedding ring when Pammie handed it to me and Judge Raines said: "This is why we never do these ceremonies over storm drains!" We had a reception at a private home following Mass.

In the closing prayer John Coleman worked in a quote from Molly Ivins, for which Pat has continued to tease him mercilessly, as unable, scholar that he is, to even say a prayer without a footnote!

On Sunday, Pat's 4 nephews moved him into my apartment. Initially, he didn't understand why we couldn't live in his 400 sq. foot apartment at the Tate Mason, suggesting I "get rid of all your old stuff and move in with me?" I explained it was not my wish, nor my right, to rid myself of my Grandparents' antiques and art. I was merely this generation's steward. Besides, I could not survive in his small space, one of my two bedrooms was a framery where I earned part of my living, and I did need some closet space. He caved and moved into my place.

Our marriage has been wonderful, though our first two weeks had an awkward tone I found difficult to understand. Nothing went wrong, but I kept expecting it to. I found it almost impossible to trust that Pat was who he had appeared to be. I was, unwittingly, waiting for a shoe to drop. It never did, never has.

My Jesuit-trained husband turned out to be totally ideal. I am the envy of all my girlfriends. Despite that initial unexpected, unprepared-for dinner, he turns out to be an excellent cook. In fact cooking has become his hobby. He prepares dinner every night, does buttermilk pancakes on Sunday morning. He does his own laundry, vacuums, mops the kitchen floor, picks up after himself and helps me make the bed each day. Once I came home from work to find Paddy standing at the ironing board in the kitchen ironing the sheets and pillow cases. I asked in amazement, "What are you *doing*?" He knew I liked such things that Gran did, he said, so was starching and ironing them all. Every woman should be so lucky.

We started out a little iffy. Monday after the wedding day, Paddy's first whole day in my apartment, we went out to lunch, bra shopping and later to a movie. Before the movie a classic guy flick, "Gladiators," Paddy asked if I needed anything at the Tacoma Mall. My underwear was a bit raggedy and I could really use a new bra. Pat offered to pay, saying "I think that's my job now."

We meandered into Macy's. I left him, I thought, on the main floor, catching the escalator to the second floor women's lingerie section. I hadn't gone 10 feet when I heard a very loud call, "What size brazier do you wear? These are 'D' cups. Is that you? What's a cup?" I hadn't heard the word "brazier" since the 50's! Isolated from women's shopping, my dear Paddy,(as I have since always called him) accidentally dated himself. Two elderly women clerks near the cash register giggled. I explained he was quite new to bra shopping. Still, He absolutely insisted on helping, as I pleaded with him to wait for me on the first floor; no way was he welcomed in the dressing room.

That first day, after lunch out, bra shopping, dinner and a movie: We arrived home late, shortly after 10:00. I was exhausted, having had only 1 day off work. I began brushing my teeth and getting ready for bed. Pat said, "What are you doing?" "Getting ready for bed. I'm really sleepy, aren't you?"

"You can't go to bed yet; the chores are not done!" "What chores?" "Before we left, you turned on the dishwasher. It needs to be emptied." "I'll empty it in the morning, after breakfast."

"But I can't sleep until the chores are done." "I can. You hide and watch."

I went to bed, conking out immediately. An hour or so later Pat came to bed, having searched my fairly large kitchen to determine where to put the clean dishes, pots, pans, glassware and silverware.

On Tuesday, before I even got up, Paddy had re-arranged my entire kitchen, moving the pans, dishes, glassware, dried goods, spices, everything. When he was done, he proclaimed, hands on hips: "Now then! You stay out of my kitchen. You'll fuck it up!"

Our legal wedding day was June 3, 2000. In October, Pat received word from Pope John Paul II that he had permission to marry in the church. I cooked a special Sunday dinner. My son, Morgan, Pat's brother and sister-in-law and Paul Fitterer all gathered again in front of our fireplace. We married all over again.

Some months after the wedding, some high school friends of Paddy's invited us to dinner: Dick and June Kennedy and Eddie and Geri Allen. During dinner they were all grousing that Seattle Prep was naming to the Athletic Hall of Fame a less than stellar athlete in Paddy and Eddie's class. Thinking I was aware of Paddy's past, I piped up: Wasn't Paddy an outstanding athlete? He tells me he was number one on Prep's Golf Team. Eddie began laughing uproariously. Eddie said, "Did Pat tell you that? Pat was the only one **ON** the golf team." More laughter and a sheepish look on Paddy's face. **BUSTED!!!**

Among other gifts to me and many, Paddy writes. He wrote a poem for our wedding. He writes little ditties on Christmas cards and birthday cards and Valentines. One of my favorites is this poem that Paddy, reflecting on his many years as a single, Jesuit priest, now married, wrote for me on our second anniversary:

> I had not known before such love . . . not this
> Where every day the same face first is seen,
> Where evening ends and morning starts with kiss
> Profound, though sometimes, strange, forgotten
> By neglect. Had not known arm and leg
> And heart entwined so close, so fragile too,

That every word, each phrase, all thought must beg
For patience, understanding, empathy anew.
I never knew what daily love required
Nor its rewards, nor ever hoped to know,
Till I wed you, and most deep desired
Into that knowledge desperately to grow.

So, though I know not yet all love-life's rule,
Still, these have been two wondrous years of school.

I especially treasure a poem Paddy wrote for me on a Mother's Day years ago when I was struggling with my relationship with a now very adult son. I felt so deeply that my love for Morgan had been ineffective, unappreciated, even fruitless. Our relationship survived, miraculously, and now thrives, but I needed this poem at that time:

No measuring mother's love by what's
Returned, nor by rewards nor gratitude.
When water inundates the ground, it still
Might fallow stay. Strong counter winds deter
An arrow's flight. Even best planned roads
May not to Rome arrive, nor every prayer
Bring solace sought. Voluminously
Lavished love, abounding hope
Might yield slight fruit or modest blossom
However green parental gardener's thumb.
Still, love, because all that is in you must
Your child to God's abundant grace entrust.

The rest is a long series of miracles. Paddy has been hospitalized for his heart and/or admitted for "Procedures," in and out of the Emergency Room, collected on a gurney from home, sent to Harborview now a totally of 51 times since our wedding. But, thanks be to God, he is still with us. He has had to give up golf, tennis, bowling and long walks, but is still one heck of a terrific chef! He is also thoughtful, loyal, helpful around the house, a terrific laundress, great meal planner, congenial with my friends. I could go on for hours about the privilege of being married to Pat Carroll, but many reading this have known him much longer than I have, so no surprises; just Lucky Me!!

A Marriage Not Without Hiccups

To be honest, however, our marriage has not been without a few hiccups. Most married couples argue about sex and money. We don't. We argue about the laundry. Over and over and over and over. Paddy felt, since he had a new title, "husband", that he should participate, help with EVERYTHING!...au contrere...there are a few things I wanted to do my self....ALL BY MYSELF; i.e., the laundry.

For openers, Paddy didn't understand (nor believe) the dryer shreds lingerie. Having moved out of his family home at 18 into the Jesuit Community, he had never been in a position to know that washing womens' clothing and underwear is very different from washing men's.

I asked him, if he insisted doing laundry, if he would please just do HIS laundry. That worked for a week. After that, he began removing my laundry from my personal laundry basket throwing my laundry in with his because there was wasted space in his wash, his personal laundry was so small.

We argued about that procedure for more than two years. In addition, paddy has a penchant for bleach. He insisted everything needed to be bleached to keep the colors bright. (Someone told him that years ago. He memorized it!)

Paddy never liked using the "bleach" receptacle....the triangular box at the entrance of the washer on the right hand side that says "Liquid Bleach Here". He relished holding the bleach bottle about 6" over the clothes, while pouring half a LARGE bottle of bleach DIRECTLY on the clothes! Watching him do it nearly gave me a stroke!

The second Christmas after we married I bought him a beautiful set of royal blue towels and a rug for his blue bathroom.

The next thing I knew they showed up on Paddy's "laundry day" with HUGE white splotches all over his beautiful royal blue towels and rug. I asked him why he had poured the bleach directly on the towels, since the bleach basically destroys their appearance. Paddy said, "I don't mind the spots". Eyes bugged out and mouth dropped open, I just stood there. There was no possible response.

The bleach saga continues to this day....Paddy doesn't mind wearing khakis and other clothing with large bleach spots. He doesn't understand why I object to multiple bleach spots on my clothes, which I have had to throw away. Since he still insists on washing my clothes, too, I have had to check the bags whenever he comes home from the store, when he is not looking, for bleach. I also check the laundry room regularly for errant bottles of the same. In the past many years, at least ten, I can't begin to enumerate how many bottles of bleach I have discovered, snuck out of the house, and thrown away.

On occasion, I hear Paddy say, "Have you seen that bottle of bleach I brought home yesterday?"

"No, Paddy. Did you accidentally leave it in the car, since it was likely too large to fit into the grocery bag?" I try to work up an innocent a sounding voice. So far, so good.

Adjustments – All Married People/Partners/ Roommatess Must Make Adjustments

All wedded people or partners residing together need to adjust - but some surprises/adjustments are more shocking than others. At least I walked into this marriage thinking/hoping Paddy was pretty close to perfect; no nasty mother-in-law to deal with (Paddy's step-mother, Edith, was a dream); no children from his first marriage to hate me, as he was a Jesuit; no enormous spousal and child support that we had to pay....everything looked pretty smooth....

....until one night, SPLAT!!! In a hurry, I quickly pulled a bottle of Italian salad dressing out of the fridge......all over our linoleum floor in our Edgewater Apartment! Turns out Paddy doesn't believe in screwing on/replacing tops of bottles, jars, cans, boxes anything else...it is nearly impossible to clean oily dressing off of linoleum; especially linoleum that is over 30 or 40 years old, maybe older. It took me a good hour and a half on my hands and knees.

Paddy carefully (and quite seriously) explained to me the purpose of screw tops, lids and caps: It is, he said, to keep litter or dirt/ dust from falling in. "There is no need to screw the caps on", he said, "It's a waste of time!"...I do notice, however, he does carefully screw the top on Scotch bottles!

I should have learned from that gentle lecture to be oh, so careful in the future of anything with a top..........

What never crossed my mind were cartons: sour cream cartons, for instance. I'm not even going to mention how mad I was when I pulled a 1-pound carton of sour cream out of the fridge, only to find the top was "gently placed" across the top, causing the carton to buckle when I picked it up, crash to the linoleum floor with an-other SPLAT!

....I'm not going to bring up how long it took me, on my hands and knees again, to scrape, scour, scrub it off the floor; nor will I mention the fact that I was furious all afternoon, muttering and sputtering until paddy got home from work.....his explanation, of course, was: "There's no need to fasten lids....all you have to do is place them on top of containers so nothing falls in."

He actually said that with a straight face, looking right at me, believing what he was saying.

I won't bring up the fact that when the Catsup jar hit the floor, it bounced twice, splashed not only the floor, but the front of the fridge, my clothes and all the cupboards across from it! No, I don't think I'll mention that because, to this day, it still makes me mad. I won't even bring it up! I was partially culpable because my hands were wet when I reached for the jar, but REALLY???..not even the catsup bottle deserves a fastened top?

Fool me once, shame on you; fool me twice, shame on me; but how dumb do I feel, having been surprised a couple dozen times? It took me at least a year to learn a new way of picking up jars, cartons *and* containers of all sorts and sizes.....adjustments....all partners must make adjustments.......

The final event was one morning, in my sleepy 7:00 a.m. fog, I shook the carton of High Pulp orange juice before breakfast...good thing I hadn't had my shower yet, as I had orange juice in my hair, all over my white terry robe and on the kitchen ceiling!...okay, I finally got it!...never, ever do anything with ANYTHING that has a top, a screw-top jar lid, or a carton . I got it....took me a year or two to get all the "tops" figured out, but Paddy finally had me trained! He used to say, pointing at me, "You can't train one of these," but he did!

On the lighter side, I trust Paddy, with all of his Theological training, multiple Masters Degrees and Jesuit experience, to answer my religious "Dogma?" questions with some authority. I miss my pets, especially Alice, Mazel tov, and Rasky. I asked Paddy, "When we get to Heaven, do we get our pets back?"

Scratching his chin with head cocked, he replied, "deedeemac, (he calls me deedeemac) I don't know for sure about our pets, but what I DO know for sure is if we are very good on earth, we get all our sox back!"

Wrap up

I have spent most of my life believing other people were more valuable than I while I was exhausted trying to catch up. I know now it's okay to just be myself. Everyone else is taken, after all!

A simple story from my professional life, usually donning a tool belt all day long: One working day, I was installing art at Bonney-Watson's new Funeral Home near Sea-Tac – an enormous new facility. All day long, as I climbed ladders and pounded posts into the walls, People were pushing gurneys up and down the hall, painting faces on cadavers, preparing to bury the several deceased persons there that day.

At the end of a long day, as I stood on the couch in the entrance, installing a large painting over the sofa, I heard two women talking at the reception desk, believing me out of range to hear them. The funeral home accountant said to the receptionist: "Isn't it strange what that woman does for a living?"

I love my strange work. I am grateful for it every day. A further word of gratitude before I leave:

I am grateful for Pat Carroll; a husband who is kind, thoughtful, funny, a brilliant conversationalist, over-educated (with three Masters Degrees), a wonderful companion, spiritual, a voluminous reader, disciplined, patient, helpful in home chores, loyal, warm, non-critical, a talented editor and gifted writer (with 9 books to his name) and a fabulous cook!....and that's just for openers.

I am grateful for Gran and Grandfather who adopted me in 1942. They took upon themselves the role of my parents when Grandfather was 71 and Gran 49. They taught me what love looks like. And what it feels like.

I am grateful for my Jesuit Parish community – many loving, caring, compassionate people we see every Sunday and often at celebrations, Masses and dinner gatherings in between.

I am grateful for a small group of friends who have stood by me through all of my traumas and especially the poverty-stricken single mother era, friends who have been with me since the early sixties and, some, even years before that.

I am grateful for Madison Park, the small town I live in – a place where I run into friends when I walk to the grocery, pharmacy or bakery; friends who say "Let's grab a cup of coffee"; a place where I can watch the children on the slides and swings in the park next to our fabulous WPA tennis courts; where I can watch families with their dogs on the beach; where I can get a haircut, take out Thai food, have my clothes cleaned, buy sandpaper at the hardware store and make a bank deposit (where all the Tellers call me by name) all in the same short walk.

I am grateful for my son, Morgan, who, though having experienced traumas of his own, including the divorce of his parents, has grown into an intelligent and good man of stringent ethical and moral standards, with an enormous heart – a heart his friends and family can count upon whenever needed, a fabulous role model for his football team. I am grateful for Morgan, but also extremely proud to be the mother of a son who has grown into such a fine man. He will be an exceptional father/husband/family man someday.

I am grateful for perfect health so I can still play tennis 2 or 3 times a week and *not* use the elevator in our condo to access the third floor from the basement garage.

I am grateful for the truth of my friend Nancy Clark's assessment: "Aren't you glad you lived long enough to thrive in a good marriage?" Nancy, you have no idea!

I am no longer an inconvenience, but rather a convenient, necessary and integral part of a good life. Thank you to everyone who has befriended me, encouraged me, nurtured me, been patient with me and prayed for me these nearly 8 decades. Life is good.

Overwhelmed with blessings, I echo what Paddy says, "Thanks for all that has been; yes to whatever will be."

Feeding My Spirit

The Rosary is an ancient Catholic custom, popularized since 1214 by Saint Dominic. I have a favorite pink Rosary, I purchased three years ago in Rome at the Vatican. It consists of 55 one-quarter inch pink beads, all carved like roses; 4 small imitation gold medals, each engraved with a different Italian Basilica. Those are the "Our Father" beads; an oval medal engraved with Pope Francis and a Crucifix.

When I took night classes from Father Joe Kramis in the '70's, I learned about the Rosary. The rosary, for Catholics, is similar to the mantras most world religions have -- to quiet and center oneself.

The Rosary is a magic potion for me. It only takes 20 minutes, preferably in the morning, to set my day on a happy and peaceful course. My attitude all day is noticeably different when I remember to set aside those few minutes. I am much more patient with Paddy, Morgan and clients. Those are the days I don't get parking tickets because I lack the patience to park a block away and hoof it!

There are specific blessings/graces to ask for on the 10 decades ("Hail Mary") beads between each of the "Our Father" medals. For instance, prayer requests for "Social Justice", "Patience in Adversity", "Hope" and many more.

The way I say the Rosary is I have a small blue paper,(2" x 3"), book Father Joe gave me in the '70's (which can still be purchased at "Kauffer's Religious Supplies") that lists word-by-word instructions on how to say the Rosary. I still follow it each day because it is too much information for me to recall!

At the end of the Rosary, I kneel beside my bed, as Gran taught me, in prayers of petitions and gratitude, for all the good things I have been given, including Paddy, Gran, Grandpa and Morgan, the Davidson family, the Davidson-Nolz family, my St. Joseph Parish, our faithful First Chance Board, a few cherished friends, perfect health and professional work that I love in the arts.

And last I pray for social justice, for our teens at the Academy, especially the homeless students with little ones, and the middle schoolers at the Nativity School; the committed faculties and staffs who love, educate and nurture them. I also pray for the many thousands of struggling people under Father Greg Boyle's watchful, inclusive tender care and love; (what he terms "The no-matter-whatness of

God"); the terrible racism and injustice in our beleaguered country; I pray for my friends who are struggling with cancer, financial hardship, unwanted divorces, family conflicts and mental illness. God and I have very specific conversations. God is my Good and Best Friend.

My friend, Marilyn, confided to me once that her bedtime petitions for her friends and family became so long that she finally just said, "And now, God, please refer to my list!" I will close with some of my favorite maxims:

1. "You don't need another person, place or thing to make you whole. God already did that. Your job is to **know it**."...**Maya Angelou**

2. "I'm fully convinced the greatest thing you can do for someone; the most Jesus-like, most God-honoring thing is to err on the side of loving them."...**Maya Angelou**

3. "In the end, the most important thing is not to do things for people who are poor and in distress, but to enter into relationship with them, to be with them and help them find confidence in themselves and discover their own gifts" ... via **Gregory Boyle, S.J.**

4. "**Before** you speak to me about your religion, first show it to me in how you treat other people;

   Before you tell me how much you love your God, show me how much you love all his children;

   Before you preach to me of your passion for your faith, teach me about it through your compassion for your neighbors.

   In the end, I'm not as interested in what you have to tell or sell as how you choose to live and give.".…**Cory Booker**

5. **Mother Theresa** didn't worry about her thighs;

   She had shit to do!

6. "Service is the rent we pay for being. It is the very purpose of life; not something you do in your spare time".…..**Marian Wright Edelman**

7. "There is no strength but kindness".…**Gregory Boyle, S.J.**

8. "Not all of us can do great things. But we can do small things with great love…**St. Teresa of Calcutta (Mother Teresa)**

9. "People are often unreasonable and self-centered. Forgive them anyway.

   If you are kind, people may accuse you of ulterior motives. Be kind anyway.

   If you are honest, people may cheat you. Be honest anyway.

   If you find happiness, people may be jealous. Be happy anyway.

   The good you do today may be forgotten tomorrow. Do good anyway.

   Give the world the best you have and it may never be enough. Give your best anyway.

   For you see, in the end it is between you and God.

   It was never between you and them anyway."

   …**Mother Teresa**

10. "If you want to be a true professional,

You will do something outside yourself;

There are tears are in your community;

Something to make life a little better for people less fortunate than you;

That's what I think is a meaningful life –

Living not for oneself, but for one's community"

…Justice Ruth Bader Ginsburg

Justice Ginsburg also says **"Well behaved women rarely make history!"**

11. "You is kind;

You is important;

You is smart."

…..Aibileen Clark….from the movie **"Help"**

12. Be the kind of woman who, when your feet hit the ground in the morning, the devil says:

"Oh crap! She's up!"

dee McQuesten and Pat Carroll...Wedding Day June 3, 2000

*Mayor Paul Schell and Pam Schell at residential wedding
reception....Paul read the Gospel for the Wedding Mass...
Pam was Matron of Honor....June 3, 2000*

Pat Carroll at 70th Birthday Party...2006

Paddy's Forever Family: Christopher Staeheli, Anita Staeheli,
Mike Hagan-Murphy, Julia Hagan-Murphy, Pat Carroll,
Kathleen Douglas, Reimer Douglas…Quilcene, 2017

Pat Carroll and Suzie Callison Dicks...Hood Canal....2019

With a grateful heart, many, many thank you's go to friends and family who have held me up by the elbows to muddle through the writing of this tome:

My husband, Pat Carroll, who took a "lump" of written material and arranged it into chapters with sub-headings and tossed the stories he didn't like;

Jon Nolz, who sat with me for hours to insert the photos and faithfully gave me on-call technical computer advice on the phone and in person for months;

Polly Kenefick, Maureen Thomas, Shannon Hoffer, Kaaren Andrews, Christopher Staeheli, and Pam Schell; each of whom slogged all the way through the original manuscript, to give me immeasurable valuable opinions and advice.

Time spent with treasured friends has become more and more dear...Carolyn and Eddie Baker surprised us one sunny summer afternoon with a "Proper English Tea"....2018

Sailing Puget Sound on the Atalanta!

dee McQuesten Skippering the Atalanta on Puget Sound!...2018

THESE ARE THE ARMS OF CLAN MACDONALD OF SLEAT,
OF WHICH McQUISTON IS A SEPT.

McQuesten Family Crest

The first shadow box I made after I established McQuesten
Framing & Fine Art Service, almost 30 years ago. These are family
photos I placed around the flapper gown Gran McQuesten made
for Governor Hartley's Inauguration Ball in 1926 during the time
Grandpa McQuesten was in the Washington State Senate

My Installation Crew hanging tapestries in Madrona...2018

Restoration Project: Smoke removal from an ancient painting…2018

Installation Crew hanging large oil paintings in a steep stairwell....2019

*Burnley Snyder and Pat Carroll at Richard Weisman's
dinner to view his Andy Worhal Collection...2015*

Cousin Paul Fitterer's Farewell Mass at Seattle Prep...2018

Newly cleaned and restored ancient oil painting in a beautiful hand-made frame made especially for this piece of art…2017

When I have huge frames and art to deliver, I rely on Penske....
Parking their big trucks is a lot of fun in downtown Seattle!

On Paddy's 51st hospital and/or "Outpatient Event", Father
Glenn Butterworth and Bob McCaffrey-Lent brought us
Mass to Paddy's hospital room...March, 2020

Thanks to Anne Farrell, we have discovered Petanque!

The steel balls to play Petanque!

Pearl Jam, on one of our most complicated art installations,
hired us to install their favorite Touring Posters in their
stairwell....12' wide and 16' high...it took 9 hours

Fifteen percent (15%) of the profits from this book will be donated to First Chance Industries, a 501c3 (and divided equally between them)

1. The Nativity School, an Independent Jesuit-Endorsed STEM Middle School for impoverished at-risk children is located in Central Seattle. (The Nativity School, a totally scholarship-funded student body, (depending 100% upon donations) seeks to break the cycle of poverty through an education that nourishes hearts and ignites leaders for love and service.)

2. The Academy in Seattle's Columbia City for traumatized/marginalized high school students from toxic environments, seeking a High School Diploma; many of whom are homeless, have infants and toddlers of their own, and are on Supervised Probation.

3. Homeboy Industries in Los Angeles, the largest gang rehabilitation program in the world designed to love, nurture, rehabilitate, educate and employ both men and women extricating themselves from gangs, coming out of incarceration and other traumatic lifestyles; founded and headed by Jesuit Father Greg Boyle.

Website for the Nativity School: www.seattlenativity.org

Website for First Chance Industries & Academy:

www.firstchanceindustries.com/

Website for Homeboy Industries Los Angeles:

www.homeboyindustries.org

Photo by Kathleen Douglas